بسم الله الرحمن الرحيم

"It is not righteousness that you turn your faces
Towards east or West, but it is righteousness - to
believe in Allah and the Last Day, and the Angels,
and the Book, and the Messengers; to spend of your
substance, out of love for Him, for your kin, for
orphans, for the needy, for the wayfarer, for those who
ask, and for the ransom of slaves; to be steadfast in
prayer and practice regular charity; to fulfill the
contracts which you have made; and to be firm and
patient, in pain and adversity, and throughout all
periods of panic. Such as the people of truth,
the God-fearing."

(Qur'an Surah al-Baqara, 2:177)

Presented to ....

From ....

Date ....

THE MORAL VALUES OF THE QUR'AN

HARUN YAHYA

Goodword
B·O·O·K·S

First published 1999
© Goodword Books 2001
Reprinted 2001, 2002

GOODWORD BOOKS
1, Nizamuddin West Market
New Delhi 110 013
Tel. 435 5454, 435 6666, 435 1128
Fax 435 7333, 435 7980
E-mail: info@goodwordbooks.com
www.goodwordbooks.com

Contents

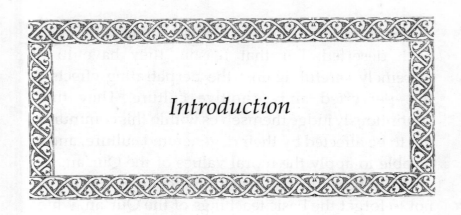

Introduction

The moral values of the community we live in are rather distorted. These moral principles which are the products of selfish passions and the greed of people, yield then to selfishness, arrogance, sarcasm, rudeness and cruelty. People believe that, in order to improve their living standards they have to cheat or deceive others.

However, these are not the values that Allah has determined for the human beings He created. The Qur'an orders people to be dignified, modest, trustworthy, kind, faithful, mature and responsive. The Qur'an even describes the way we should walk: Turn not your face away from men with pride, nor walk in insolence through the earth. Verily, Allah likes not each arrogant boast" *(Surat Luqman, 31:18)*

On that account, duty of a believer is to apply these superior principles that Allah has decreed.

Yet, today believers live in will be renoved a

miscreant community where these divine ethics have been deserted. For that reason, they have to be extremely careful against the perpetrating effects of this perverted and primitive culture. They must continuously judge themselves within this community not to be affected by their degenerated culture, and to be able to apply the moral values of the Qur'an.

This brochure has been prepared to help believers not to forget the basic teachings of the Qur'an, which they should always keep in mind.

In the following pages, these moral principles and prayers that are likely to be forgotten by the believers will be examined in the light of related verses of the Qur'an.

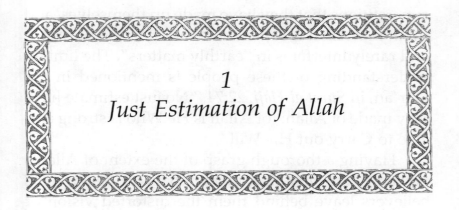

1
Just Estimation of Allah

The Qur'an informs us of the true attributes of Allah:

"Allah! There is no god but He, the Living, the Self-subsisting, Eternal. No slumber can seize Him nor sleep. His are all things in the heavens and on earth. Who is there can intercede in His presence except as He permits? He knows what (appears to His creatures as) before or after or behind them. Nor shall they compass aught of His knowledge except as He wills. His Throne does extend over the heavens and the earth, and He feels no fatigue in guarding and preserving them for He is the Most High, the Supreme (in glory)." (Surat al-Baqara, 2:255)

"Allah is He Who created seven heavens, and of the earth the like of them; the decree continues to descend among them, that you may know that Allah has power over all things and that Allah indeed encompasses all things in (His) knowledge." (Surat at-Talaq, 65:12)

However, most people not perceiving Allah as He is described in the above verses, cannot comprehend His eternal power and greatness. They believe in

9

superstitions that they have made up themselves, and think that Allah is somewhere far off in the universe, and rarely interferes in "earthly matters". The limited understanding of these people is mentioned in the Qur'an, in *Surat al-Hajj*, 22:74. "No just estimate have they made of Allah: for Allah is He Who is strong and able to Carry out His Will."

Having a thorough grasp of the extent of Allah's power is the first link in the chain of belief. True believers leave behind them the distorted vision of Allah prevailing in their community, and deny these perverted beliefs by saying: "There were some foolish ones among us, who used to utter extravagant lies against Allah." *(Surat al-Jinn*, 72:4)

The faithful believe in Allah in the way the Qur'an describes. They examine the signs of Allah in both external and internal worlds, and thus begin to understand the great art and power of Allah.

But if the believers happen to overlook Allah and fail to ponder deeply on Him and on His Creation, they may start to be influenced by immoral beliefs particularly at times of difficulty. Allah mentions this as a potential risk in the verse of *Surat Aal-e-Imran*, 3:154, about the believers who gave up during the war, and "who were anxious on their own account, thought wrongly of Allah, the thought of ignorance."

A believer would never like to make such a mistake, therefore he should free his heart from everything that appertains to the beliefs of the ignorant, and accept this real faith with all his heart in the way the Qur'an describes.

10

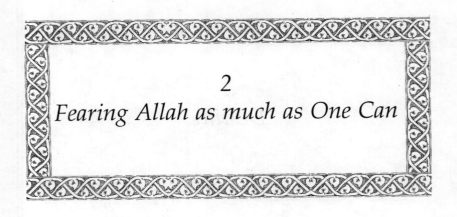

2
Fearing Allah as much as One Can

To fear Allah is the beginning of all. The more one fears Allah, the more superior does one become in the presence of Allah. The Qur'an gives the examples of the prophets, with whom the believers can compare themselves so that they may understand that they really can increase their fear of Allah.

Allah wants people to fear Him to the greatest possible extent. Various ways of showing reverence for the Almighty can be found, for example; spending in Allah's way, doing good deeds, taking the prophet as an example, obeying him, being attentive to the rules of Allah etc.

"So fear Allah as much as you can; listen and obey and spend in charity for the benefit of your own soul. Those saved from the covetousness of their own souls, are the ones that achieve prosperity." (Surat at-Taghabun, 64:16)

"O you who believe! Fear Allah as He should be feared, and die not except in a state of Islam." (Surat Aal-e-Imran, 3:102)

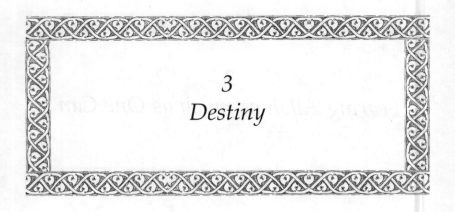

3
Destiny

Nothing in the universe is accidental. As it is stated in the Qur'an: "He regulates all affairs" (*Surat ar-Ra'd*, 13:2). In another verse it is said: "Not a leaf falls but with His knowledge." (*Surat al-An'am*, 6:59). It is Allah Who creates and directs all the events; how they will begin and how they will end. It is again Allah Who determines every movement of every star in the universe, every state of every living thing on Earth, the way one will live, what one will say, what one will encounter, as expressed in the verses:

"*Verily, We have created all things with Qadar (Divine Preordainments of all things before their creation)*" (*Surat al-Qamar*, 54:49)

"*No misfortune befalls on the earth or in yourselves but is inscribed in the Book of Decrees, before We bring it into existence. Verily, that is easy for Allah.*" (*Surat al-Hadid*, 57:22)

The believers should be aware of this great reality,

and in consequence, should never act ignorantly as those who deny it. Having understood that life is just "following destiny", they never become disappointed or feel afraid of anything. They become confident and firm as the Prophet Muhammad, who told his companion, "Be not sad, surely Allah is with us." (*Surat at-Tawba*, 9:40) when the latter was apprehensive about being found in the cave by the idolaters who wanted to kill them.

4
Putting Trust in Allah

Since Allah is the only decision-maker, every happening is in favor of the believers: everything has been planned for the benefit of religion and for the believers' life in the hereafter. Believers can refer to their past experience to see that there is a good for them at the end of every event. For that reason, believers put their entire trust in Allah. He is the one and only Protector. What a believer should do is to behave as Allah wants him to: fulfilling his responsibilities but depending on Allah for the outcomes. The following verses express this mystery, which is unknown to unbelievers.

"... for those who fear Allah, He (ever) prepares a way out. And He provides for him from (sources) he never could imagine. And if any one puts his trust in Allah, sufficient is (Allah) for him. Verily, for all things has Allah appointed a due proportion." (Surat at-Talaq, 65:2-3)

"Say: 'Nothing will happen to us except what Allah has

14

decreed for us: He is our Protector: and in Allah let the believers put their trust.'" (Surat at-Tawba, 9:51)

What the believers should say to the unbelievers is also stated in the Qur'an:

"And why should we not put our trust in Allah while He indeed has guided us our ways. And we shall certainly bear with patience all the hurt you may cause us, and in Allah (alone) let those who trust, put their trust. (Surah Ibrahim, 14:12)

In another verse, it is said:

"If Allah helps you, none can overcome you; and if He forsakes you, who is there after Him that can help you? And in Allah (Alone) let believers put their trust." (Surat Aal-e-Imran, 3:160)

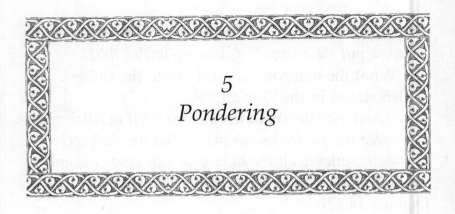

5
Pondering

In the Qur'an, it is stated that the unbeliever is one who neither recognizes nor appreciates the signs of Allah. The distinguishing mark of a believer is his ability to see those signs and proofs. He knows that these are not created in vain, and can realize the power and great art of Allah everywhere and find ways to revere Him. He is one of those men of sense, who "celebrate the praises of Allah, standing, sitting, and lying down on their sides, and contemplate the (wonders of) creation in the heavens and the earth, (and say): 'Our Lord! not for naught have You created (all) this! Glory be to You! Give us salvation from the penalty of the Fire.' " *(Surat Aal-e-Imran, 3:191)*

At various points in the Qur'an, expressions like, "will you not take heed?", "...there is a sign for thinking men," lay stress on the importance of pondering upon the signs of Allah. Allah has created an endless list of subjects for reflection. Everything we see and sense in the heavens and on the earth and in

16

between is indeed a manifestation of Allah's creativity and, as such should be food for thought. One of the verses gives the example of these divine blessing of Allah:

"With it He produces for you corn, olives, date palms, grapes and every kind of fruit: verily, in this is a sign for those who give thought." (Surat an-Nahl, 16:11)

Let us think for a moment of one of the above mentioned items: the date palm. The tree, as is well known, grows up from a seed out of the earth. From this tiny seed (a seed is not even 1 cubic centimetre in size), arises an enormous wooden mass of 4-5 metres long and hundreds of kilograms in weight. The only thing that the seed can use while constituting this great mass is the earth in which it is buried.

How can a seed know how to form a tree? How can it "reason" to decompose the necessary substances in the soil to create wood? How can it predict the required shape and structure? This last question is especially important, because it is not an ordinary wooden piece that emerges from the seed. It is a complex living organism with roots for assimilating substances from the earth, with veins and with branches that are perfectly organized. A human being has difficulty in drawing even a picture of a tree, while on the contrary a simple seed can produce such an extremely complex object by merely using the substances in the soil.

This observation concludes that a seed is extremely intelligent and wise, even more so than we are. Or to

17

be more precise, there is an amazing intelligence in what a seed does. But what is the source of that intelligence? How can it be possible for a seed to have such intelligence and memory?

No doubt, this question has a single answer: the seed is created by being endowed with the ability to form a tree, that is, it is programmed so in advance. Every seed on earth is encompassed by Allah and grows within His knowledge. In one of the verses it is stated:

"With Him are the keys of the unseen, the treasures that none knows but He. He knows whatever there is on the earth and in the sea. Not a leaf falls but with His knowledge: there is not a grain in the darkness (or depths) of the earth, nor anything fresh or dry (green or withered), but is (inscribed) in a record clear." (Surat al-An'aam, 6:59)

It is Allah who creates the seed and causes it to spring forth as a new plant. In another verse it is said:

"It is Allah Who causes the seed-grain and the date-stone to split and sprout. He causes the living to issue from the dead, and He is the one to cause the dead to issue from the living. That is Allah: then how are you deluded away from the truth?" (Surat al-An'aam, 6:95)

The seed is merely one of the numerous signs that Allah has created in the universe. If men begin to think not only with their minds but also with their hearts, and ask of themselves, the questions "why" and "how", they will be able to understand that all of the universe is the proof of the existence and power of Allah.

18

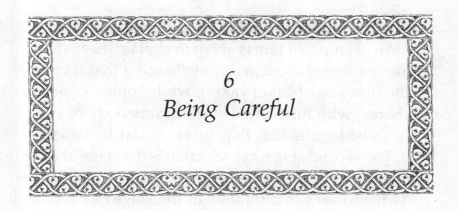

6
Being Careful

As we stated at the beginning, Allah created the universe to show the signs of His Creation.

However, the unbelievers cannot understand this fact since they do not have the ability to "see" this divine purpose. As the Qur'an expresses it: "They have eyes with which they do not see." (*Surat al-Araf*, 7:179). With their materialistic vision, they do not have the wisdom and comprehension to grasp this important reality.

Believers are quite different from this "blind" category, because they realize and accept that the whole universe is created by Allah with a certain aim and wisdom. This belief is the first step of faith. As faith and wisdom increase in parallel with each other, they will begin to be able to identify every detail of Allah's Creation.

In the Islamic tradition, progress in faith is in three steps: ilm-el yakin (being informed), ayn-el yakin (seeing), and Hakk-el yakin (experiencing).

An example of rain is given to explain these steps. There are three stages in acknowledging that it rains. In the first stage (ilm-el yakin), while someone sits in his home, with his windows shut, somebody coming from outside tells him that it rains, and he believes him. The second stage, ayn-el yakin is the stage of eye-witnessing. The person goes to the window, opens the curtain and sees that it rains. In the stage of Hakk-el yakin, he opens the door, goes out of the house, and there he is; "in" the rain.

Being careful is a prayer in action to proceed from the stage of ilm-el yakin to the stage of ayn-el yakin and even more.

Seeing the signs of Allah and not being "blind" like the unbelievers, require a high degree of concentration. In the Qur'an, the believers are called to observe and notice the signs of Allah around them and this is only possible by being careful:

"See you the seed that you sow in the ground? Is it you that cause it to grow, or are We the Cause?" (Surat al-Waqia, 56:63-64)

"See you the water which you drink? Do ye bring it down (in rain) from the cloud or do We?" (Surat al-Waqia, 56:68-69)

And Allah states in another verse that the blind could not be held equal to the seeing and asks "Will you then consider not?" (*Surat al An'am, 6:50*)

One should train oneself to recognize the signs of Allah and should always keep them in mind. Otherwise, the mind will start to wander, jumping from one topic to another, wasting time in thinking about useless things. This is a kind of unconsciousness; you cannot control your mind when you lose your consentration in Allah. You cannot focus on a subject. Indeed, you cannot conceive the truth behind events, nor can you ever have the competence to affect the course they take. On the contrary, your mind is directed by stray happenings. You are "bewildered" all the time, which is not the attribute of the believer, but of the unbeliever.

"... if anyone assigns partners to Allah, it is as if he had fallen from heaven and been snatched up by birds, or the wind had swooped and thrown him into a far-distant place." (Surat al-Hajj, 22:31)

Believers, on the other hand, are the ones who direct their minds better to perceive Allah, and who try in better ways to serve His religion. They free their minds from any vain thoughts, and whenever they become aware of the appeal of Satan, they rescue themselves, just as is described in the Qur'an:

"Verily, those who are the pious, when an evil thought comes to them from Satan, they remember Allah, and (indeed) they then see (aright)." (Surat al-A'raf, 7:201)

Therefore, the believers should be careful to keep their minds free of useless thoughts, and never lose the thread of what is happening around them, they should always be on their guard.

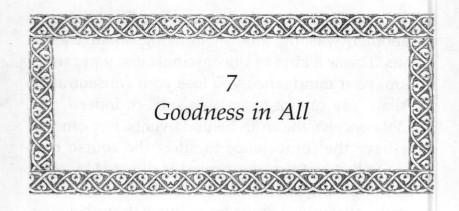

7

Goodness in All

All things are created with wisdom and with an ulterior purpose. In consort with this ulterior purpose, there are benefits for the believers in all happenings. Because Allah is on the believers' side and does not let them down.

Encounters in life may at first seem unfavorable for the believers. However, one should understand that even seemingly dire events, for example, a plot of hatched against them by the unbelievers, will ultimately turn out well for them. Allah will sooner or later let them savour His beneficence so, believers should be completely sure that there is goodness in all.

There are many examples of this kind of situation in the Qur'an; the life of Yusuf (Joseph) is one of the most remarkable. In his childhood, Yusuf had been thrown down to the bottom of a well by his brothers. He was later rescued and then accused and imprisoned, even though he was innocent. For a person without faith, these incidents may be thought of as the greatest misfortunes. Nevertheless, Yusuf always kept in mind that these could only happen under Allah's direction and that all would certainly turn out for the better. And this proved to be true. Allah turned the "disasters" to good account; Yusuf was released from prison and in time became one of the governors of that land.

The situation with Yunus (Jonah) was no different. He fled to a laden ship, where, to retain his place, he drew lots. When the draw proved unfavourable, he was thrown into the sea where he was swallowed by a gigantic fish. The Qur'an informs us that he was rescued and was sent to a "nation a hundred thousand men or more," only because he had glorified Allah.

"Had he not been of them who glorify Allâh, He would have indeed remained inside its belly (the fish) till the Day of Resurrection. But We cast him forth on the naked shore while he was sick, And We caused a plant of gourd to grow over him. And We sent him to a hundred thousand (people) or even more. And they believed; so We gave them enjoyment for a while." (Surat as-Saaffat, 37:143-148)

All these examples given in the Qur'an teach us that the events which seems to be a "misfortune" are not really so for the believer. If he puts his trust in Allah, seeks refuge in Him and asks help only from Him, then nothing will be a matter of regret for him. Allah does create certain difficulties, but they are only to put man to the test and to strengthen believers' loyalty and faith.

The opposite holds true for the unbelievers.

Nothing in this life can be good for them. Things that strike them as delightful or pleasant are indeed "misfortunes", and these will increase their torment in the Hereafter. Anything that they achieve unjustly is entered in their record, and for this they will ultimately be responsible. On this score the Qur'an records Allah's commandments:

"And let not those who covetously withhold of that which Allah has bestowed on them of His Bounty think that it is good for them. Nay, it will be worse for them; the things which they covetously withheld shall be tied to their necks like a collar on the Day of Resurrection. And to Allah belongs the heritage of the heavens and the earth; and Allah is Well- Acquainted with all that you do." (Surat Aal-e-Imran, 3:180)

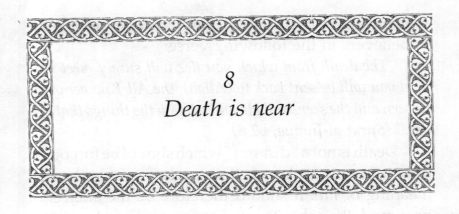

8
Death is near

The members of the profane society are basically ignorant, negligent and shallow. Their lives are not based on common sense or logic. On the contrary, they live with vain and false beliefs, and follow conjectures that end with fallacies. One of these is their belief about death. They believe that death is something even not to be thought about.

What they really expect is to escape from it by ignoring it. By not thinking about it, they believe that they can elude it. But this is just like the ostrich who puts her head in the sand in order to escape from the danger. Ignoring danger does not make it disappear. On the contrary, the person at risk will certainly encounter danger, but without having made any preparations for it, will, in consequence receive a much bigger shock— unlike the believers who ponder on and prepare themselves for this important reality, the truth of which has been experienced by all the people

25

who have ever lived. Allah, therefore, admonishes the unbelievers in the following verse:

"The death from which you flee will surely meet you, then you will be sent back to (Allah), the All-Knower of the unseen and the seen, and He will tell you the things that you did." (Surat al-Jumua, 62:8)

Death is not a "disaster" which should be forgotten, but an important lesson that teaches people the real meaning of life. It should therefore be the subject of profound thought. The believers ponder deeply on that great reality with sincerity and wisdom. Why do all people live for a period of time and then die? All created beings are mortal, and this shows that they are powerless and unable servants of Allah. Allah is the only owner of life; all creatures have come to life by Allah's Decree and will ultimately die by Allah's Decree. On this the Qur'an declares: "All that is on earth will perish: But will abide (Forever) the Face of your Lord,- full of Majesty, Bounty and Honour." (*Surat ar-Rahman,* 55:26,27)

Everyone will die, but none can predict where and when that will be. Nobody has any guarantee that he will be alive the next minute. Therefore believers should behave as if they are to die at any moment. Thinking about death will help believers increase their sincerity and fear of Allah and they will always remain conscious of what awaits them.

In the Qur'an, the significance of keeping death in mind is expressed in the following verse:

"We granted not to any human being immortality

26

before you, then if you die, would they live forever? Every soul shall have a taste of death: and We test you by evil and by good by way of trial. To Us you will be returned." (Surat al-Anbiya, 21:34-35)

9
The Never-Ending Attempts of Satan

When Allah created Adam and commanded the angels to prostrate themselves before him, they all prostrated themselves except Satan, who thenceforward was cursed. Satan's response was to ask Allah for a reprieve till the Day of Resurrection. This was so that he would have the opportunity to make people transgress. Once reprieved by Allah, he committed himself to a course of action intended to derail mankind:

"He said: 'Because You have sent me astray, surely I will lie in wait against them (human beings) on Your Straight Path. Then I will come to them from before them and behind them, from their right and from their left, and You will not find most of them as thankful ones'" (Surat al-A'raf, 7:16-17)

"'I will mislead them, and I will create in them false desires; I will order them to slit the ears of cattle, and to change the nature created by Allah.' Whoever, forsaking Allah, takes satan for a friend, hath of a surety suffered a loss

that is manifest." (Surat an-Nisa, 4:119)

One who is unaware of the menace of Satan, cannot protect himself against him and can easily be deceived by him. Therefore, believers should be fully alert to Satan, as is commanded in the Qur'an:

"Verily Satan is an enemy to you: so treat him as an enemy. He only invites his adherents, that they may become Companions of the Blazing Fire." (Surah Fatir, 35:6)

Those who should be the most cautious about Satan are the believers, because it is they who are Satan's actual targets. There is no need for him to try to make the unbelievers transgress; because they have already turned out to belong to his own army. He, therefore, strives to the utmost to weaken the believers so as to prevent them from serving Allah. That is why believers are particularly warned against Satan:

"O you who believe! Follow not Satan's footsteps: if any will follow the footsteps of Satan, he will (but) command what is shameful and wrong: and were it not for the grace and mercy of Allah on you, not one of you would ever have been pure: but Allah doth purify whom He pleases: and Allah is One Who hears and knows (all things)." (Surat an-Nur, 24:21)

As Allah says in the Qur'an, true believers will not be affected by the activities of Satan. But those who are weak and heedless may be easily influenced by his delusions. Never should we forget that Satan is ceaselessly striving to promote evil. Believers should always be on their guard and keep Allah in mind at all times.

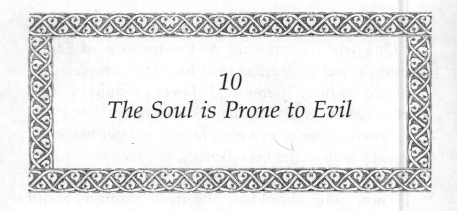

10
The Soul is Prone to Evil

Another enemy that we should guard against is within ourselves. Allah has inspired in people both good and evil. The evil inspiration in us always works for Satan. The Qur'an explains the two sides of our souls:

"By the soul and Him Who perfected it in proportion and inspired it to understand what is right and wrong for it. Truly he succeeds that purifies it. And he fails that corrupts it!" (Surat ash-Shams, 91:7-10)

People should be aware of this evil in themselves and always be on guard against the danger. Denying this evil side of our souls will not help us to escape from it, and we should try to purify it as is laid down in the Qur'an.

Believers should never, therefore, claim that they are entirely pure, but be wary of the vain provocation of their souls. The admission of Yusuf (Joseph): '"Nor do I absolve my own self (of blame): the (human) soul is certainly prone to evil, unless my Lord bestows His Mercy: but, surely, my Lord is Oft-forgiving, Most Merciful,'" (*Surah Yusuf*, 12:53) should always be borne in mind as a good example of the appropriate attitude.

People should carefully watch out for the foibles of the soul and do good and practice self-restraint, as in another verse it is averred that "men's souls are swayed by greed." *(Surat an-Nisa*, 4:128) What that greed may lead men to, is also stated in the Qur'an. It was the soul of one of Adam's sons that prompted him to murder his brother: "The (selfish) soul of the other led him to the murder of his brother: he murdered him, and became (himself) one of the lost ones." (*Surat al-Ma'ida*, 5:30). It is the same propensity to evil that made Samiri lead Moses' people astray in his absence. Samiri says "...thus did my soul suggest to me." (*Surah Ta-Ha*, 20:96)

The only way to attain salvation is by curbing the evil of the soul:

"Those saved from the covetousness of their own souls, they are the ones that achieve prosperity." (Surat al-Hashr, 59:9)

"And as for him who fears to stand in the presence of his Lord and forbids the soul from low desires, the Garden will be his home." (Surat an-Nazi'at, 79:40-41)

The struggle with one's soul is the biggest struggle for a believer. The believer has to check upon himself to decide which of his emotions and wishes are acceptable and which are evil. He has to stand against the evil instigations of his soul such as selfishness, jealousy, arrogance and greed.

Our souls shall cause us to entertain vain desires and passions. They whisper to us that we will be satisfied when we gain more money, and to have a higher status. However, these pleasures never satisfy the believer in any real sense. The more money we have, the more we will want to have. In many ways, our souls will lead us to act just like insatiable wild animals.

Our souls can only be satisfied if we devote ourselves to Allah, and not to our own shallow desires. We are created to be the servants of Allah: "...for without doubt in the remembrance of Allah do hearts find satisfaction." (*Surat ar-R'ad*, 13:28). Nothing else can give peace and satisfaction.

That is why only true believers have completely satisfied souls, because they keep themselves away from evil, guard against the depravity of their souls and dedicate themselves to Allah.

"To the righteous soul the Almighty will say: 'O soul, in (complete) rest and satisfaction! Come back to your Lord, well pleased (yourself), and well-pleasing unto Him! Enter you, then, among My devotees! Enter you my Heaven!'" (Surat al-Fajr, 89:27-30)

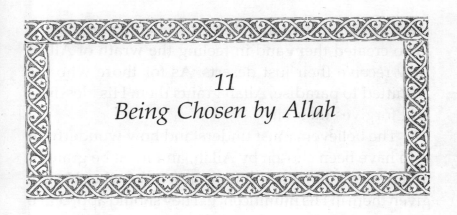

11
Being Chosen by Allah

If we cannot determine our physical appearance, neither can we determine our destiny. It is only Allah Who determines the birth of a man, his community, his family and the experience he will have throughout his life. It is again Allah Who inspires in us wisdom and good sense.

Even our faith in Allah does not depend on our own characteristics. Again it is Allah, the One and Only, Who grants us faith. He is the One Who guides, teaches and trains. As Musa (Moses) said in reply to a question put by Pharaoh: "Our Lord is He that gave to each thing its form and nature and further, gave guidance." (*Surah Ta-Ha*, 20:50)

Therefore, believers are the ones who have been singled out for Allah's favour: "Your Lord creates and chooses as He pleases: no choice have they (in the matter)" (*Surat al-Qasas*, 28:68)

Those who go to hell are the people who fully

deserve it, because they have rebelled against Allah Who created them and in feeling the wrath of Allah, they receive their just deserts. As for those who are admitted to paradise, Allah grants them His blessings and forgives their sins.

The believers must understand how wonderful it is to have been chosen by Allah, and must be grateful and praise Allah with all their hearts for what He has given them in His munificence. They should appreciate that they have been chosen from among millions of people and that they are the few blessed servants of Allah to be selected and set apart from a community whose members face perdition. The entire conduct of the believers should reflect the honour of this great privilege. Allah describes those who face perdition thus:

"By (the Token of) Time. Verily man is in loss. Except those who have faith and do righteous deeds, and recommend one another to truth, and recommend one another to patience" (Surat al-'Asr, 103:1-3)

Is there a higher honour than that of being rescued and exalted above all others by the Lord of the Universe?

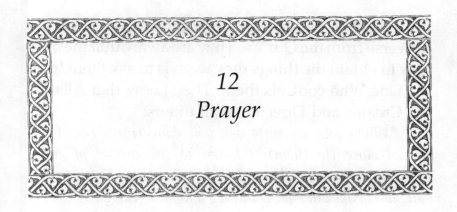

12
Prayer

In one verse, the importance of prayer is stated thus: "Say: My Lord would not care for you were it not for your prayer" (*Surat al-Furqan*, 25:77)

Prayer is the way to call on Allah; indeed, it is one of the most important characteristics that distinguish a believer from an unbeliever. Prayer is a significant indicator of one's faith in Allah.

Most of the people may think that there is no divine control on the universe and everything is interacting independently. However, what they do not know is that every soul in the heavens and on the earth has already submitted to Him; there is no creature whose destiny is not determined by Allah and who is not obedient to Him. When He decrees a thing, He only says, "Be," and it is (*Surat al-Baqara*, 2:117).

The unbelievers do not understand this substantial fact and spend their whole life by trying to affect this universe made up of imaginary matters. The believers, on the other hand, learn this great mystery of the universe from the Qur'an. They are aware that the only way to obtain the things they want is to ask them from the One Who controls them. They know that Allah is the Creator and Director of all things:

"When My servants ask you concerning Me, I am indeed close (to them): I listen to the prayer of every suppliant when he calls on Me: Let them also listen to My call, and believe in Me: That they may be led aright." (Surat al-Baqara, 2:186)

However, it should also be understood that Allah's answering to prayers is not necessarily gibing all that is wanted from Him. For man is ignorant and he "prays for evil as he prays for good; for man is ever hasty." (*Surat al-Isra,* 17:11) So Allah answers to all our prayers, but sometimes gives what is wanted, and sometimes not, since it is in truth, "evil".

The way we should pray is also defined in the Qur'an: with humility and in private, in all sincerity, having hope but also fear of Allah in our hearts, and with strong concentration:

*"Call on your Lord with humility and in private: ....,
call on Him in fear and hope: for the Mercy of Allah is always near to those who do good." (Surat al-A'raf, 7:55-56)*

In another verse it is said that "the most beautiful names belong to Allah: so call on Him by them" (*Surat al-A'raf*, 7:180)

Our prayers are actually a matter of confessing our weakness while showing our gratitude towards Allah. Abstaining from prayer shows arrogance and rebellion against Allah. Allah states in His book:

"Call on Me; I will answer your prayer: but those who are too arrogant to serve Me will surely find themselves in Hell - in humiliation!"(Surat al-Ghafir, 40:60)

Calling on Allah is both a prayer and also a great blessing. This very simple act of making a request is the key to attaining all physical and spiritual objectives.

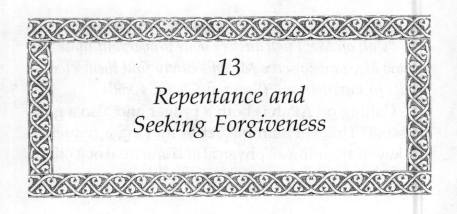

13
Repentance and Seeking Forgiveness

Two of the most repeated names of Allah in the Qur'an are, "Compassionate" and "Merciful". Allah is very truly merciful to His servants and does not punish them at once for their sins:

"And if Allah were to seize mankind for their wrongdoing, He would not leave on it (the earth) a single moving (living) creature, but He postpones them for an appointed term and when their term comes, neither can they delay nor can they advance it an hour (or a moment)." (Surat an-Nahl, 16:61)

By reprieving them, He gives wrongdoers time to ask for forgiveness and to repent. No matter how important the sin one commits, one always has the opportunity to be forgiven if one repents and behaves righteously:

"When those who believe in Our signs come to you, Say: 'Peace be on you: Your Lord has written Mercy for Himself, so that, if any of you does evil in ignorance, and

thereafter repents, and amends (his conduct), then surely He is Oft-forgiving, Most Merciful." (Surat al-An'am, 6:54)

Repentance also includes an appeal for support and strength from Allah to help the wrongdoers not to repeat the same misdeeds. The form of repentance accepted by Allah is one that is followed by good deeds: "And whoever repents and does good has truly turned to Allah with an (acceptable) conversion" (*Surat al-Furqan, 25:71*)

Sometimes an individual may commit the same sin as a result of his soul's provocation, even after repentance. But this is not an excuse for him not to repent again. He may repent for his evil deeds all throughout his life. And it should be remembered that, it will not be accepted only if one repents when death comes and one begins to dread one's fate in the Hereafter.

"Allah accepts the repentance of those who do evil in ignorance and repent soon afterwards; to them Allah will turn in mercy: for Allah is full of knowledge and wisdom."(Surat an-Nisa, 4:17)

"Of no effect is the repentance of those who continue to do evil, until death faces one of them, and he says, 'Now I have repented indeed', nor of those who die rejecting Faith: for them have We prepared a punishment most grievous." (Surat an-Nisa, 4:18)

Another verse calls all the believers to salvation: "Believers! turn all together towards Allah, so that you may attain Bliss." (*Surat an-Nur, 24:31*)

14
Patience Till Death

People are created impatient, and, as a result, make various mistakes. However, religion requires everyone to be patient for the sake of Allah. Believers, in particular, should patiently await the great salvation that Allah promised. This is how the believers are commanded in the Qur'an: "Be patient for the sake of your Lord" (*Surat al-Muddaththir*, 74:7). Patience is indeed one of the most important qualities in the struggle to reach Allah; it is the virtue one should cultivate in order to be closer to Him.

"O you who believe! Persevere in patience and constancy; vie in such perseverance; strengthen each other; and fear Allah; that you may prosper." (Surat Aal-e-Imran, 3:200)

In the community of the ignorant, the real meaning of patience is mixed up with endurance. However, endurance has a very different message which is forbearing against pain or distress. Yet, patience is entirely different as described in the Qur'an. This difference can only be comprehended by the believers. The perseverance of the believer is for gaining the pleasure of Allah. Therefore, if gives delight to the believers, whilst "endurance" gives only annoyance and distress to the unbelievers. The Qur'an expresses this as: "Seek (Allah's) help with patient perseverence and prayer:It is indeed hard, except to those who bring a lowly spirit." (*Surat al-Baqara*, 2:45)

Another verse from the same surah emphasizes the glad tidings to be given to those who are patient in the face of obstacles or difficulties.

"Be sure we shall test you with fear and hunger, some loss in goods or lives or the fruits (of your toil), but give glad tidings to those who patiently persevere, who say, when afflicted with calamity: 'To Allah We belong, and to Him is our return.'" (*Surat al-Baqara*, 2:155-156)

Patience is such a superior characteristic that it can increase the strength of the believers. Allah reveals in below verse how strength may increase with respect to patience:

"For the present, Allah has lightened your (burden), for He knows that there is a weak spot in you: But (even so), if there are a hundred of you, patient and persevering, they will vanquish two hundred, and if a thousand, they will, with the leave of Allah, vanquish two thousand, for Allah is with those who patiently persevere." (*Surat al-Anfal*, 8:66)

Patience is, moreover, a quality that subsumes all the other positive characteristics described in the Qur'an. A person may be modest, humble, generous,

41

obedient or devoted; but only when he combines these virtues with patience, will they be of worth. It is the patience shown in the prayers and the attributes of believers, that makes them acceptable.

Patience pervades the whole life of the believers, who obey the decree: "Be patient for your Lord's sake." Finally, Allah takes their souls and rewards them with His Paradise. Angels at the gates bid welcome to the righteous, saying: "Peace be on you for that you persevered in patience: Now, how excellent is the final home!". *(Surat ar-Ra'd*, 13:24)

15
Support by Allah

In profane society, people develop their characters according to the power or status they possess. For the individual to be self-confident, he must be either very rich or famous, or beautiful or handsome. Being the son or daughter of a "respected" man is also an important reason for self-confidence in a purely ignorant community.

However it is quite a different matter for the believers. This is because the believers rely for support on no one but Allah, attach no importance to any of the worldly criteria that the unbelievers follow.

Allah is always the supporter of the believers. He never lets them down in the face of opposition from the unbelievers. "Allah has decreed: 'It is I and My messengers who must prevail'" (Surat al-Mujadila, 58:21), so the messengers and those who follow them will triumph with this great support. Allah guarantees: "If they intend to deceive you, Allah is sufficient for you. He it is Who has strengthened you with His help and with the believers." (*Surat al-Anfal*, 8:62)

It should never be forgotten that it is only Allah who strengthens and improves the believers and enables them to succeed. It is not enough just to depend on physical cause and effect. These can achieve nothing, except being prayers in action. Of greater avail is verbal prayer, for it is in response to prayer, that Allah produces the desired results. That is why the believers have to rely solely on the support of Allah.

As a result, they become so courageous and confident as to challenge the world. They become too strong to be affected by any negative thought or action. Musa (Moses), who did not lose heart while all his people transgressed, said: "If you show ingratitude, you and all earth together, yet is Allah free of all wants, worthy of all praise." (*Surah Ibrahim*, 14:8) .

Musa was that confident and fearless, because he was certain that Allah and His support were always with the believers. Allah had once revealed to him: "Fear not! for you indeed have the upper hand."(*Surah Ta-Ha*, 20:68)

Musa's attitude should definitely be an example to all the believers. For Allah has promised to protect and support not only Musa and other messengers, but all believers—every one them—against the unbelievers, and lead them to triumph. As stated in the Qur'an;

"...never will Allah grant to the unbelievers a way (to triumphs) over the believers." (*Surat an-Nisa*, 4:141)

The believers are responsible for merely

44

maintaining their devotion to Allah and being good servants of Him. When this is the case, they will have nothing to fear.

"O you who believe! Guard your own souls: If you follow (right) guidance, no hurt can come to you from those who stray; to Allah is your return, it is He that will show you the truth of all that you do." (Surat al-Maida, 5:105)

Unbelievers can never do harm to the righteous. All plans and plots made against the believers will be useless. In the verse below, this mystery is explained:

"Mighty indeed were the plots which they made, but their plots were (well) within the sight of Allah, even though they were such as to shake the hills!" (Surah Ibrahim, 14:46)

While unbelievers plot against believers, in reality Allah "draws them near to destruction by degrees from whence they know not." (*Surat al-A'raf*, 7:182). They suppose that they are superior to the believers and can easily beat them. However, Allah is on the believers' side and His Power, Glory and Greatness are manifest to them. The Qur'an expresses this truth, which cannot be comprehended by the hypocrites, as follows:

"They are the ones who say, 'Spend nothing on those who are with Allah's Messenger, to the end that they may disperse.' To Allah belong the treasures of the heavens and the earth; but the Hypocrites understand not. They say, 'If we return to Medina, surely the more honourable will expel therefrom the meaner." But honour belongs to Allah and His Messenger, and to the Believers; but the Hypocrites know not." (Surat al-Munafiqoon, 63:7-8)

This is definitely an unchangeable rule. Believers, in accordance with the verse, "O you who believe! Take your precautions..." (*Surat an-Nisa*, 4:71), shall always be careful and cautious of unbelievers, but feel the comfort of the above divine rule.

Allah explains the same rule in another verse:

"Those who reject Allah, hinder (men) from the Path of Allah, and resist the Messenger, after Guidance has been clearly shown to them, will not harm Allah in the least but He will make their deeds of no effect." (Surah Muhammad, 47:32)

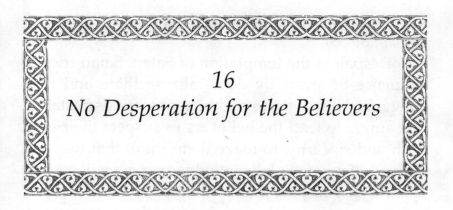

16
No Desperation for the Believers

There are two kinds of hopelessness. The first kind arises when confronted with difficulties or obstacles. Such should not be the conduct of a believer. He should always keep in mind that Allah has promised to give support to the believers. The Qur'an states that Allah is sufficient for the believers and that He has strengthened the believers with His Aid.

The second kind of despair is more dangerous, which is giving up hope of Allah's mercy after making a mistake or committing a sin. Because this may lead to the thought that Allah will not forgive one's sins and that one will necessarily go to hell. But this idea—a mere apprehension—is quite the opposite of what we are taught by the Qur'an. Indeed, Allah forgives the sins of all those who sincerely repent. It is never "too late" for seeking refuge in His mercy. Allah addresses His servants thus:

"O my Servants, who have transgressed against their souls! Despair not of the Mercy of Allah: for Allah forgives

all sins: for He is Oft-Forgiving, Most Merciful." (Surat az-Zumar, 39:53)

Despair is the temptation of Satan. Satan tries to influence believers by demoralizing them and thus dragging them down to commit more serious mistakes. His aim is to lead the believers to suspect their own faith and sincerity, to make them think that they are "fakes". If a person falls into this trap, he will start to lose his self-respect and consequently his faith, and will go on to commit bigger sins after that first mistake.

In such a state of mind, believers should immediately seek refuge in Allah, think only of Qur'an's teachings and immediately develop a new frame of mind. The Qur'an describes what the believer must do in such cases.

"And if an evil whisper comes to you from Satan, then seek refuge with Allah. Verily, He is All-Hearer, All-Knower." (Surat al-A'raf, 7:200)

If the individual is sincere in his faith in Allah, Allah forgives him even if he has made mistakes or committed sins. Furthermore, even if he has been insincere for a long time, he still has the chance to repent. It is just a trick of Satan that makes him give way to despair. For Allah is the One Who shows eternal mercy and justice and the One Who promises victory and His Paradise to the believers. The advice of Yakub (Jacob) should be a guide for all the believers:

"...never give up hope of Allah's Soothing Mercy: truly, no one despairs of Allah's Soothing Mercy, except those who have no faith." (Surah Yusuf, 12:87)

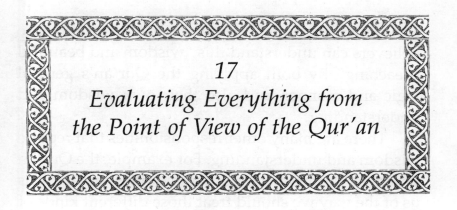

17
Evaluating Everything from the Point of View of the Qur'an

The aim of life for a believer is solely that of being a servant of Allah. People are not created to fulfill their vain desires and greed, or to pursue their passions; the one and only reason for our creation is to serve Allah.

The way to achieve this is by taking the Qur'an as our unique guide. We should give all our attention to applying every decree of the Qur'an. Our target should be to observe every decree of the Qur'an as much as possible.

We can see from the Qur'an that the responsibility of the believers rests not only on decisive verses, such as those on regular prayers, fasting or hajj but also on prayers that require interpretation. For instance, in one verse believers are urged to "invite (all) to the Way of their Lord with wisdom and beautiful preaching; and argue with them (unbelievers) in ways that are best

49

and most gracious" (*Surat an-Nahl*, 16:125). The believers can understand this "wisdom and beautiful preaching" by both applying the Qur'an's general logic and manner, and also their own wisdom and understanding.

There are many other responsibilities that require wisdom and understanding. For example, the Qur'an describes various models of communities, and informs us of the way we should treat those different kinds of people. And what should be said to those people is mostly mentioned in the Qur'an in the verses beginning with, "Say...".

The verses that advise believers how to behave are clearly described in the Qur'an. But if these precepts are to be applied to daily life, instant recognition of their true significance is a must. At this point, it is the wisdom and understanding of the believers that help.

The Qur'an describes various kinds of people, such as believers, Christians, Jews, hypocrites and pagans. We must learn the concerned verses very well, because what actually should be done is to identify those kinds of people in our society and act towards them as the Qur'an commands. This is inevitable for being a "living Qur'an".

Moreover, believers should realize that all the people around us undoubtedly belong to one or more of the categories of people described in the Qur'an. All the people exist to form the society described in the Qur'an and none is created in vain:

"Not for (idle) sport did We create the heavens and the

earth and all that is between!" (Surat al-Anbiya, 21:16)

However, it is not only the people around us that are described in the Qur'an. In fact, everything that we see and everything that happens are indeed reflections of what is written in the Qur'an.

"Soon will We show them our Signs on the horizons, and in their own souls, until it becomes manifest to them that this is the Truth. Is it not enough that your Lord witnesses all things?" (Surah Fussilat, 41:53)

The whole universe consists of signs of Allah. Just like a painting presents its painter to the on-lookers, just like every detail on this painting shows the brush prints of the painter, all the universe and every detail of this universe exist to present Allah, the Creator of all things. The more believers realize this fact, the more will they recognize Allah and painstakingly obey all His decrees. As one comprehends that life with all its details, is actually a "sign" as defined in the Qur'an, one will relate everything at every stage of one's "daily life" to the values of the Qur'an.

Everything takes place in accordance with the destiny Allah has determined and therefore, everything has a purpose. What believers should do is interpret each event in the light of the Qur'an and react in the way the Qur'an prescribes. For example when encountered with something "vain" and idle, the believer should pay no heed to it. But the fact is; this vain thing is already created so that the believer pays no heed to it. The believers should interpret every happening according the perspective of the Qur'an.

So, they actually must develop their culture and characteristics in conformity to the Qur'an, how Allah decrees. In order to achieve this, they must leave all they have attained from their ignorant past and society. They should decide what to do in every circumstance by depending on the interpretation and logic of the Qur'an, because, the words of Allah show them the way to handle each situation. As it is said in the Qur'an, it was sent down to us as a Book "explaining all things" (*Surat an-Nahl*, 16:88).

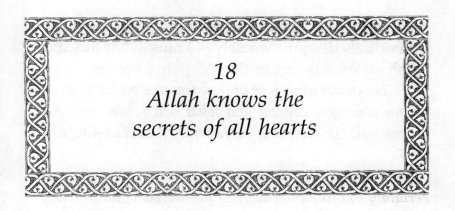

18
Allah knows the
secrets of all hearts

The most basic characteristic of the unbelievers is their insincerity. They are insincere to Allah, to other people and even to themselves. Although when they behave warmly to people in the face for the sake of their interests, they can easily feel at the same time hatred or jealousy for them. As a matter of fact, their insincerity is also to their own selves. Although they clearly witness the wrongness and evil of their deeds, they push this reality back into their subconscious and act as if they were entirely perfect and right.

At the basis of this insincerity there lies the assumption that nobody will know about the secret thoughts they have in their hearts. So, the quilty may act as if they were not so, despite their sins or wrongdoings. Actually, in an ignorant society, people really do not know what the actual thoughts of others are, and they never consider that Allah knows all the thoughts and secrets of all hearts. The subconscious mind is also included in this knowledge, even if the individuals do not themselves know what lies there. Allah states this fact in the following verses:

"He knows what is in the heavens and on earth; and He knows what you conceal and what you reveal: and Allah knows well the secrets of all hearts." (Surat at-Taghabun, 64:4)

"Whether you hide your word or publish it. He certainly has full knowledge of the secrets of all hearts. He is the One that understands the finest mysteries and is well-acquainted with them." (Surat al-Mulk, 67:13-14)

Nobody, therefore, can speak outside the knowledge of Allah, for He is the One Who has full knowledge of the secrets of all hearts. In the Qur'an, this fact is revealed as:

"Do you not see that Allah knows all that is in the heavens and on earth? There is not a secret consultation between three, but He makes the fourth among them, - nor between five but He makes the sixth- nor between fewer nor more, but He is in their midst, whersoever they be. In the end will He tell them the truth of their conduct, on the Day of Judgment. For Allah has full knowledge of all things." (Surat al-Mujadila, 58:7)

This being so, it is not possible to hide anything from Allah. Allah knows not only all the deeds but also all the thoughts of all people, including those of their subconscious, which they are largely unaware of. This is emphasized in the following verse:

"It was We Who created man, and We know what dark suggestions his soul makes to him: for We are nearer to him

54

than his jugular vein." (Surah Qaf, 50:16)

In these circumstances, the eventual behavior of the believers should be complete sincerity and modesty before Allah. Since Allah has created and already knows all beings, it is insensible to act in an artificial manner before Allah. One should sincerely uncover all one's weaknesses, faults, wrongdoing and defects in one's faith to Allah, and ask for His help and mercy.

The prophets are the best examples for their sincerity to Allah. The Prophet Ibrahim (Abraham) prays to Allah and says "Show me, Lord, how You will raise the dead." And when Allah replies: "Have you no faith?" he says "Yes, but just to reassure my heart." *(Surat al-Baqara, 2:260)* This is how the believers confess their weaknesses to Allah and ask for forgiveness only from Him. Similarly, when Allah commands the Prophet Musa (Moses): "Go to Pharaoh!" he says, "O my Lord! I have slain a man among them, and I fear lest they slay me," *(Surat al-Qasas, 28:33)* and asks for help and strength from Allah. This honesty of the Prophets to Allah show how the believers should behave.

Before one comprehends that one is weak and dependent upon Allah, one cannot attain characteristics like strength, modesty, faith and courage by only pretending to possess them, because "...man was created weak" *(Surat An-Nisa, 4:28)* in order to understand his weaknesses before Allah. Therefore, one should be very truthful and devoted to Allah and expose all one's faults and sins to Him before asking for forgiveness.

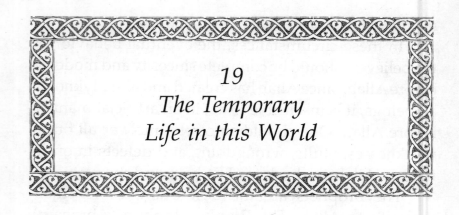

19
The Temporary
Life in this World

Man is placed on earth only for a very short time. There, he will be tested, trained and then passed over to the Hereafter where he will stay forever. The possessions and blessings of this world, although created similar to their originals in Heaven, actually possess many defects and weaknesses. For they are only intended to make man remember the Hereafter.

However, the unbelievers are not capable of comprehending this fact, so they act as if the things of this world are their sole objectives. Yet, this is wholly deceptive, since, the entirely temporary and defective favors of the world are far away from satisfying man who is created for the beauties of eternal perfection. Allah describes how the world is a temporary place full of deception:

"Know that the life of this world is only play and amusement, pomp and mutual boasting among you, and

rivalry in respect of wealth and children, as the likeness of vegetation after rain, thereof the growth is pleasing to the tiller; afterwards it dries up and you see it turning yellow; then it becomes straw. But in the Hereafter (there is) a severe torment, and (there is) Forgiveness from Allah and (His) Good Pleasure, whereas the life of this world is only a deceiving enjoyment." (Surat al-Hadid, 57:20)

Just as it is told in the Qur'an, all of the ignorant people live only for a few objectives such as riches and children and mutual boasting among themselves. In another verse the goods and chattels of deception in the world are thus described:

"Fair in the eyes of men is the love of things they covet: Women and sons; Heaped-up hoards of gold and silver; horses branded (for blood and excellence); and (wealth of) cattle and well-tilled land. Such are the possessions of this world's life; but in nearness to Allah is the best of the goals (to return to). Say: Shall I give you glad tidings of things Far better than those? For the righteous are Gardens in nearness to their Lord, with rivers flowing beneath; therein is their eternal home; with companions pure (and holy); and the good pleasure of Allah. For in Allah's sight are (all) His servants" (Surat Aal-e-Imran, 3:14-15)

The life of this world is extremely rudimentary and lacking in worth when compared to the eternal life in the Hereafter. To express this, the original Arabic word for the "world" has the connotation of a "scanty, crowded, dirty place". People consider that their 60-70 year long life on this earth will be long and a satisfying one. Yet, in a very short time death comes and all are buried in their graves. As a matter of fact, as death comes closer one realizes how short a time he has stayed in this world. On the Day of Resurrection, Allah will question the people.

"He will say: 'What number of years did you stay on earth?' They will reply: 'We stayed a day or part of a day: but ask those who keep account.' He will say: 'You stayed but a little-if you had only known! Did you think that We had created you in jest, and that you would never be brought back to Us?'" (Surat al-Mumenoon, 23:112-115)

Denying Allah and disregarding the Hereafter, in the life-long pursuit of worldly greed will mean eternal punishment in Hell-Fire. Those who conduct themselves in this way are described in the Qur'an as "people who buy the life of this world at the price of the Hereafter". For them Allah decrees: "Their penalty shall not be lightened, nor shall they be helped." *(Surat al-Baqara, 2:86)*

Another verse states:

"Those who rest not their hope on their meeting with Us, but are pleased and satisfied with the life of the present,, and those who heed not Our Signs; their abode is the Fire, because of the evil they earned."(Surah Yunus, 10:7-8)

Those who forget that this world is only a temporary place for trial and who are not careful of Allah's Signs, but are satisfied only with the worldly play and amusements of this life, assume them as their own, and even deify them will surely deserve the grevious penalty. The Qur'an describes the status of such people:

"Then, as for him who transgresses all bounds, and prefers the life of this world, then surely the hell, that is the abode." (Surat an-Nazi'at, 79:37-39)

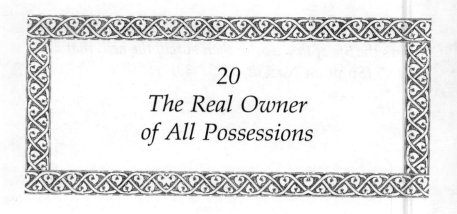

20
The Real Owner
of All Possessions

Most often, it is the fight for possessions that leads people to sorrow and pain. In fact, the entire life of the unbelievers rests upon the greed for "having property". They always struggle to have more, making this the real aim of their life.

However, this "rivalry in respect of wealth and children" (*Surat al-Hadid*, 57:20) is a total deception, since, the dominion of all possessions on earth is of Allah. People only fool themselves by thinking that they really own something, since they have neither created the things they possess, nor have they the power to keep them alive and ever-lasting. Nor can they avoid their own destruction. Furthermore, they have no status to "possess" anything, because they are "possessed" by another being. This Superior Being is "the King (or Ruler) of Mankind" (*Surat an-Nas*, 114:2) Who is Allah. The Qur'an informs us that the entire universe is possessed by Allah: "To Him belongs what is in the heavens and on earth, and all between them, , and all beneath the soil." (*Surah Ta-Ha, 20:6*). Another verse extends this to Allah, power to forgive or punish: "Do you not know that to Allah alone belongs the dominion of the heavens and the earth? He punishes whom He pleases, and He forgives whom He pleases: and Allah has power over all things." (*Surat al-Maeda,* 5:40)

As a matter of fact, Allah has given all possessions to people as a temporary "trust" in this world. This trust will last for a certain period of time and when the day of judgement comes, everyone will be asked to account for his conduct.

In this day of judgement, each one will be asked about his intentions and purpose in using this "trust" given to him. Those who considered themselves owners rather than trustees, and revolted against the Prophets by saying, "Does your prayer command you that we leave off doing what we like with our property?" (*Surah Hud,* 11:87), deserve severe punishment. The Qur'an describes what will happen to them:

"And let not those who covetously withhold of that which Allah has bestowed on them of His Bounty think that it is good for them. Nay, it will be worse for them; the things which they covetously withheld shall be tied to their necks like a collar on the Day of Resurrection. And to Allah belongs the heritage of the heavens and the earth; and Allah is Well- Acquainted with all that you do." (Surat Aal-e-Imran, 3:180)

As mentioned in the Qur'an, all the gifts given to man by Allah, by His Grace, is for him to spend with no "covetous withholding". So, instead of trying to own and preserve these possessions, one should expend them in the way Allah commands. This means that the believer will use the proper amount that is necessary for his maintenance and then spend "what is beyond his needs" (*Surat al-Baqara*, 2:219). If he does not act accordingly and tries to "keep" all his wealth, then this will mean that he sees himself as its owner. Yet, the punishment for this kind of behaviour is of a very serious nature. In the Qur'an this is explained thus:

"...And there are those who bury gold and silver and spend it not in the way of Allah: announce unto them a most grievous penalty. On the Day, when it will (all) be heated in the fire of Hell, and with it will be branded their foreheads, their flanks, and their backs. (and it will be said unto them): 'This is the (treasure) which you buried for yourselves: taste you, then, the treasures you buried'" (Surat at-Tawba, 9:34-35)

There is "economy" in Islam, but no "piling up possessions". The believers do not trust in the material things they keep or accumulate for "the bad days", but only in Allah. So, Allah increases their wealth in return. Allah gives them more than they spend in His way, and increases their blessings. This is stated in a verse as follows:

"The parable of those who spend their property in the way of Allah is as the parable of a grain growing seven ears

(with) a hundred grains in every ear. Allah multiplies for whom He pleases; and Allah is Ample-giving, Knowing." (Surat al-Baqara, 2:261)

On the contrary, the situation of the one who does not spend in the way of Allah is that of one "who piles up wealth and keeps on counting it, thinking that his wealth would make him last for ever. By no means! He will be sure to be thrown into the crushing Fire. And what will make you know what the crushing Fire is? It is the Fire of Allah kindled (to a blaze)." *(Surat al-Humaza, 104:2-6)*

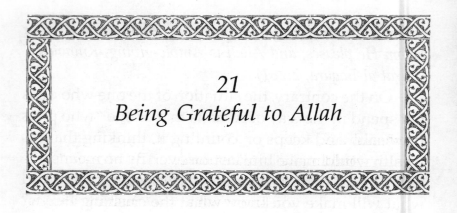

21
Being Grateful to Allah

Allah has created everything with a purpose; just like His blessings. Each one of these blessings— our life, faith, sustenance, health, eyes, and ears—is an endowment for mankind to be grateful to Allah.

Once we leave heedlessness and ignorance behind, and start to think and see with reasoning, we shall surely realize that everything around us is indeed a favour granted by our Creator Allah. All the food that we eat, the air that we breathe, all the beauties around us, in particulars, our eyes that let us see all these things — everything is a blessing of Allah. These are so numerous that the Qur'an says: "If you would count up the favours of Allah, never would you be able to number them: for Allah is Oft-Forgiving, Most Merciful." (*Surat an-Nahl*,16:18)

And, undoubtedly, all these favours are given for some reason. Nothing is created for us simply to use as we wish. On the contrary, the reason for all those favours - no matter what - is to instruct mankind towards Allah; because everything given, necessitates gratitude in return. Allah is the One Who continuously gives all the blessing; we should, therefore, show our sincere gratitude only to Him.

Gratefulness is both a great prayer and also a way to protect us from "transgressing". Without it, people have a tendency towards depravity and evil, forgetting their weaknesses and becoming haughty, the richer and more powerful they become. Showing our gratitude to Allah saves us from such "depravity". Those who show their gratefulness to Allah do so in the knowledge that everything they obtain is given by Allah, to Whom they always belong. They know that they are responsible for using these blessings in the way of Allah and only as He wills. It was this gratitude to Allah that underlay the modesty and maturity of the prophets, such as Davud (David) or Suleyman (Solomon) to whom great possessions, states and sovereignty were given. The actual problem of Karun (Qarun), who became depraved on account of his possessions, was indeed that of being ungrateful to Allah.

If a believer demonstrates that he will not become arrogant and impertinent with the blessings or riches he is given, Allah shall give him more. "...If you are grateful, I will add more (favours) unto you; but if you show ingratitude, truly, My punishment is terrible indeed." (*Surah Ibrahim*, 14:7)

Gratitude should not be shown merely with words,

it should be shown rather by utilizing each favour in a way approved of by Allah. Believers are responsible for using everything that they have been given, in the way of Allah. First of all, all the believers should start using whatever they possess, and foremost the body Allah has endowed them with, to strive for His cause. The Qur'an also informs us that we may show our gratitude to Allah by proclaiming all of His blessings, that is, by communicating His "message" to all:

"Verily your Guardian-Lord will give you (that wherewith) you shall be well-pleased. Did He not find you an orphan and give you shelter? Did He not find you wandering, and give you guidance? Did He not find you in need, and make you rich? Therefore, treat not the orphan with harshness, nor repulse the petitioner (unheard); and proclaim the bounty of your Lord!" (Surat ad-Dhuha, 93:5-11)

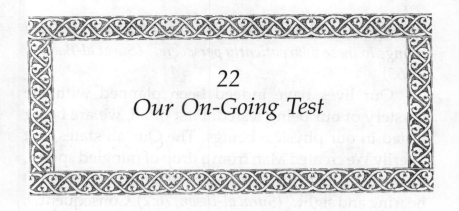

22
Our On-Going Test

As we have stated in the beginning, nothing on earth is created in vain, but rather with wisdom. Understanding this fact depends on the wisdom of people themselves. One whose faith and consequently whose wisdom and prudence increase, will happen to grasp this reasoning much better in time.

One of the most important precepts is that we are being tested throughout our whole lives. Allah tests our sincerity and our faith on different occasions. He may give favours to test whether we are grateful to Him or not. He may create difficulties, for us, to reveal whether we behave with patience or not: "Every soul shall have a taste of death: and We test you by evil and by good by way of trial. To Us you will be returned." (*Surat al-Anbiya*, 21:35)

We are to be tested in various ways. This is explained in the Qur'an in the verse below:

"Be sure we shall test you with fear and hunger, some

loss in goods or lives or the fruits (of your toil), but give glad tidings to those who patiently persevere." (Surat al-Baqara, 2:155)

Our lives have indeed been planned with the mystery of our being tested. First of all, we are being tested in our physical beings. The Qur'an states that "Verily We created Man from a drop of mingled sperm, in order to try him: So We gave him (the gifts of) hearing and sight." (*Surat al-Insan*, 76:2). Consequently, everything we hear and see is actually a part of the test. In all kinds of situations, we will be tested to see whether we behave in accordance with the Qur'an or with our own vain desires.

Allah tests the steadfastness of the believers with various difficulties. One of the most important of these is the oppression of the believers by the unbelievers. All these misdeeds, like verbal attacks, mocking, physical oppression and even torture and murder attempts, are only a means of trial for the believers. In one of the verses it is said:

"You shall certainly be tried and tested in your possessions and in your personal selves; and you shall certainly hear much that will grieve you, from those who received the Book before you and from those who worship many gods. But if you persevere patiently, and guard against evil, then that will be a determining factor in all affairs." (Surat Aal-e-Imran, 3:186)

The most important point to comprehend is that all of these deprivations and misadventures are created by Allah as a special kind of test. One who does not understand this will become very superficial. The Qur'an cites a pertinent tale of certain Jews.

"Ask them concerning the town standing close by the sea; when they transgressed in the matter of the Sabbath. For on the day of their Sabbath, their fish did come to them, openly holding up their heads, but on the day they had no Sabbath, they came not: thus did We made a trial for them, for they were given to transgression." (Surat al-A'raf, 7:163)

Only the individual who has wisdom can realize that he is being tested, and can succeed in these tests by again using his wisdom. Therefore, a believer should not forget that he is being tested throughout his life. These tests cannot be passed or the heaven cannot be attained simply by saying "I believe."

"Do men think that they will be left alone on saying 'We believe', and that they will not be tested? We did test those before them, and Allah will certainly know those who are true from those who are false." (Surat al-Ankaboot, 29:2-3)

And in another verse Allah says:

"Did you think that you would enter Heaven without Allah testing those of you who fought hard (in His Cause) and remained steadfast?" (Surat Aal-e-Imran, 3:142)

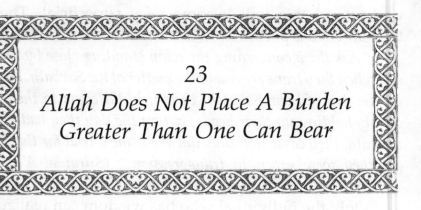

23
Allah Does Not Place A Burden
Greater Than One Can Bear

A significant portion of the community claim that it is hard for them to practise religion, and that that is the only reason they do not follow its principles. In this way they expect to lessen their guilt. But they deceive nobody but themselves.

Allah burdens no one beyond the limits of his strength. As the Qur'an says: "On no soul does Allah place a burden greater than it can bear. It gets every good that it earns, and it suffers every ill that it earns."(*Surat al-Baqara*, 2:286)

Another verse asserts that the religion that Allah has chosen for us is as easy as the religion of Ibrahim (Abraham):

"Strive in His cause as you ought to strive. He has chosen you, and has imposed no difficulties on you in religion; it is the religion of your father Ibrahim(Abraham). It is He Who has named you Muslims, both before and in

this (Revelation); that the Messenger may be a witness for you, and you be witnesses for mankind! So, establish regular prayer, give regular charity, and hold fast to Allah! He is your Protector - the Best to protect and the Best to help!" (Surat al-Hajj, 22:78)

When this is the case, it is plainly deceitful for anyone to claim that it is hard to practise religion and to put this forward as a reason for defaulting. He can deceive no one with such an explanation but himself.

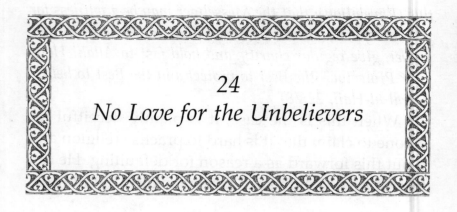

24
No Love for the Unbelievers

In order to live by the morals of the Qur'an, one should completely renounce the culture and moral values of the profane society. One of the first things to be abnegated is the understanding of love in a profane society.

In a profane society, all relations and love are based on selfish interests. One person gets along with another well only if there is some benefit to be gained from him or if he is being taken care of by the other or at least is being well-treated by him. Another measure is the family tie. People love others just because they are from the same family; or from the same dynasty, or from the same society, or sometimes even from the same nation.

However, these are not the criteria for the believers. Because believers love Allah more than anything or anyone.

"There are some among men who take for themselves

objects of worship besides Allah, whom they love as they love Allah, and those who believe are stronger in love for Allah" (Surat al-Baqara, 2:165)

Believers, respecting Allah above all else, love those who love Allah, and dislike those who disobey Him. It makes no difference whether those subject to their approval or disapproval are close to them or not. This point is elaborated in the Qur'an:

"You will not find any people who believe in Allah and the Last Day, loving (and befriending) those who resist Allah and His Messenger, even though they were their (own) fathers or their sons, or their brothers, or their kindred. For such He has written Faith in their hearts, and strengthened them with a spirit from Himself. And He will admit them to gardens beneath which rivers flow, to dwell therein (for ever). Allah is well pleased with them, and they with Him. They are the party of Allah. Truly, it is the party of Allah that will achieve felicity." (Surat al-Mujadila, 58:22)

Having even a little love for the unbelievers would never be a proper attitude for a believer. Believers are seriously warned against this in the Qur'an:

"O you who believe! Take not my enemies and yours as friends (or protectors), offering them (your) love, even though they have rejected the Truth that has come to you, and have (on the contrary) driven out the Prophet and yourselves (from your homes), (simply) because you believe in Allah your Lord! If you have come out to strive in My Way and to seek My Good Pleasure, (how) you hold secret

converse of love (and friendship) with them? I know full well all that you conceal and all that you reveal. And any of you that does this has strayed from the Straight Path"(Surat al-Mumtahina, 60:1)

The behaviour of the Prophet Ibrahim (Abraham) and those that followed him is an excellent example for all believers:

"There is for you an excellent example (to follow) in Ibrahim (Abraham) and those with him, when they said to their people: 'We are clear of you and of whatever you worship besides Allah: we have rejected you, and there has arisen, between us and you, enmity and hatred for ever, unless ye believe in Allah and Him alone' (Surat al-Mumtahina,60:4)

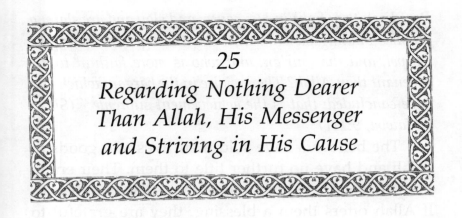

25
Regarding Nothing Dearer Than Allah, His Messenger and Striving in His Cause

The sole obligation of a believer is to serve Allah. The one and only reason for our existence is to be His servants. Life based on any other reasoning than this, means denial of the religion and worshipping idols besides Allah, which will consequently lead to Hell.

In other words, life is only a tool for a believer. He should regard every moment of his life as a means of getting closer to Allah and serving His cause. If this tool ever turns into his aim—which is indeed true of the unbelievers — he will soon find himself in great danger.

Believers live for only one cause; and that is to serve Allah, and for this they have abandoned the world. Allah explains this as:

"Allah has purchased of the believers their persons and their properties; for theirs (in return) is the garden (of

Paradise): they fight in His cause, and slay and are slain: a promise binding on Him in truth, through the Torah, the Gospel, and the Qur'an: and who is more faithful to his covenant than Allah? Then rejoice in the bargain which you have concluded: that is the achievement supreme." (Surat at-Tawba, 9:111)

The believers have sold their lives and goods to Allah and have no further title to them. Their entire lives are conducted in the way that Allah commands. If Allah offers them a blessing, they are grateful to Him, and when He commands them to strive in His cause, they do not feel a moment's hesitancy, even if they know that they are going to their deaths.

Such believers do not shirk any form of self-sacrifice and nothing on earth can prevent them from struggling for Allah's cause. They are able to leave behind all the beautiful blessings of Allah and can give up their very lives without any hesitation. On the contrary, the opposite behavior would be the sign that they had not sold their goods and lives to Allah as yet. Such a deficiency in faith will be marked down against them in the life to come.

"Say: If your fathers, your sons, your brothers, your mates, your kindred, the wealth that you have gained, the commerce in which you fear a decline, or the dwellings in which you delight are dearer to you than Allah, or His Messenger, or striving in His cause then wait until Allah brings about His decision. Allah guides not the rebellious." (Surat at-Tawba, 9:24)

This faith was so strong in the companions of the

76

Prophet Mohammed that, not only did they never refuse to fight, but there were some, on the contrary, who even wept when they did not have the opportunity to go into battle along with Mohammed. In the verse below, Allah explains the difference between the sincere and the half-hearted:

"There is no blame on those who are infirm, or ill or who find no resources to spend (on the cause), if they are sincere (in duty) to Allah and His Messenger. No ground of complaint can there be against the good-doers: Allah is Oft-forgiving, Most Merciful. Nor (is there blame) on those who came to you to be provided with mounts, and when you said "I can find no mounts for you", they turned back, their eyes streaming with tears of grief that they had no resources to spend (on the cause). The way (to blame) is only against those who ask permission of you though they are rich; they prefer to stay with the those who remain behind: Allah has sealed their hearts; so they know not." (Surat at-Tawba, 9:91-93)

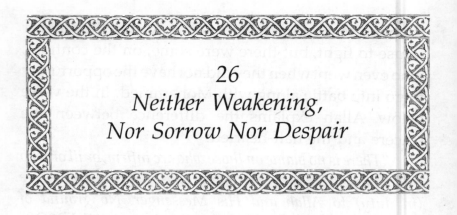

26
Neither Weakening,
Nor Sorrow Nor Despair

The believers have a long and hard struggle in the way of Allah. Their path may beset by enemies, many in number, and better equipped. However, so long as they follow Allah's Way, the believers inevitably overcome these enemies.

One of the reasons for their victory is that, as believers, they carry out this struggle with great enthusiasm and excitement. This is something that unbelievers cannot do; because, being devoted to this life, they are unfaithful to Allah. They have fears and weaknesses, and immediately give up when confronted with difficulties. On the contrary, believers never weaken since they know that Allah is always with them and they will be the ones to succeed. This is described in the Qur'anic verse below:

"Many a Prophet fought (in Allah's Cause), and along with him (fought) large bands of religious learned men. But they never lost heart which did befall them in Allah's Way,

nor did they weaken nor give in. Allah Loves those who are firm and steadfast." (Surat Aal-e-Imran, 3:146)

However, believers need to pray for this enthusiasm and excitement, for it is easy to fall a prey to faint-heartedness - something for which Satan strives very hard. At a moment of crisis, the hypocrites said to the companions of the Prophet Mohammed: "O people of Yathrib(al-Madinah)! There is no stand (possible) for you (against the enemy attack)! Therefore go back!" (*Surat al-Ahzab*, 33:13), thus trying to create a feeling of despair and bring about a consequent defeat. But the believers are warned in the Qur'an about all these dubious factors: "So patiently persevere: for verily the promise of Allah is true: nor let those shake your firmness, who have (themselves) no certainty of faith." (*Surat ar-Rum*, 30:60)

The believer is responsible only for himself and should not be affected by the weaknesses of others. Neither should the strength of enemies affect and frighten him. The whole life of believers is for Allah and they will go on praying for His good pleasure till the end of their lives. In one verse, it is decreed:

"So lose not heart and nor fall into despair: you shall have the upper hand if you are true in Faith." (Surat Aal-e-Imran, 3:139)

"Slacken not in following up the enemy: If you are suffering hardship, they are suffering similar hardships; but you have hope from Allah, while they have none. And Allah is full of knowledge and wisdom." (Surat an-Nisa, 4:104)

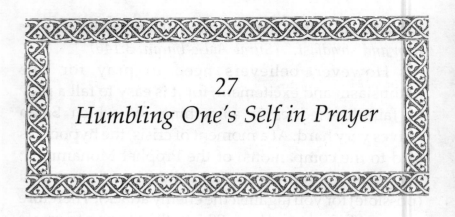

27
Humbling One's Self in Prayer

Prayer is very important since it is the visible expression of man's being a Muslim. However, The Qur'an expresses disapproval of such prayer as is offered without sincerity:

" *Woe to the praying ones, who are unmindful of their prayers; Those who (want but) to be seen (of man)."* (Surat al-Maun, 107:4-6)

That means that what makes our regular prayers proper is not the actual movements, e.g. bowing, prostrating oneself, etc., but their aim and the kind of thought given to them. Some people pray just to show others that they are "Muslims," but instead of gaining ground with Allah, they are committing a great transgression.

What gives our prayers rectitude is our consciousness that we are prostrating ourselves before Allah only in order to express our devotion to Him. That is why Allah commands believers to "stand before Allah in a devout (frame of mind.)" *(Surat al-Baqara, 2:238)*

Another verse describes the believers as "those who offer their prayers with all solemnity and submissiveness." *(Surat al-Mumenoon, 23:2).* Solemnity in this verse means experiencing fear accompanied by deep respect and having one's heart filled with awe. Such a prayer increases one's faith and closeness to Allah. It keeps man standing firm.

In another verse regular prayers are described:

"Recite the what is sent of the Book by inspiration to you, and establish regular prayer: for prayer restrains from shameful and unjust deeds; and remembrance of Allah is the greatest (thing in life) without doubt. And Allah knows the (deeds) that you do." (Surat al-Ankaboot, 29:45)

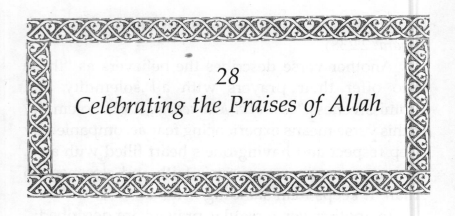

28
Celebrating the Praises of Allah

All topics of faith that we have mentioned till now, require a complete devotion to Allah, to live and to struggle for Him. This dedication cannot be attained unless there is a close contact with Allah and the way to it, is through "remembering and turning to Allah". Believers should remember their Creator, always, praise Him and turn to Him in repentance as commanded in the Qur'an: "Believers! Celebrate the praises of Allah, and do this often." (*Surat al-Ahzab*, 33:42)

This is what will make the believer "a companion of Allah" just like the Prophet Ibrahim (Abraham).

Accordingly, the believers should be grateful to Allah for the favor given to them, and ask for repentance from Allah for their evil deeds. Moreover, they should call on Allah for everything they need and praise Him as often as they can.

"*Bring your Lord to remembrance in your (very) soul, with humility and in reverence, without loudness in words, in the mornings and in the evenings; and do not be of those who are unheedful." (Surat al-Araf, 7:205)*

It is expressed thus in another verse: "...and remembrance of Allah is the greatest (thing in life) without doubt...." *(Surat al-Ankaboot, 29:45)*. Without remembrance of Allah, all prayers would lose their value. If these prayers are not performed by remembering Allah and seeking for His good pleasure, then they may be turned into unpaid deeds. When the Qur'an informs us about the attributes of the prophets, it emphasizes how they turn to Allah. In the 30th verse of *Surah 38 (Sad)*, Allah says, "to Dawud (David) We gave Sulaiman (Solomon) - How excellent in Our service! Ever did he turn (to Us)!" of the Prophet Ayub (Job), Allah says: "Truly, We found him full of patience and constancy. How excellent in Our service! Ever did he turn (to Us)!" *(Surah Sad, 38:44)*

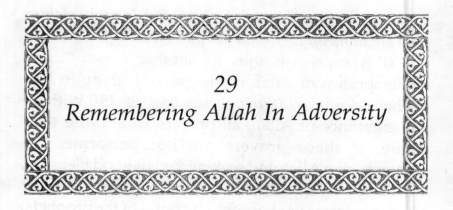

29
Remembering Allah In Adversity

Life's goal for a believer is to worship Allah. One of the most significant ways of worshipping is done through communicating Allah's message to people everywhere, and struggling against the companions of Satan. This struggle is usually very severe and harsh because most of the time "the companions of Satan" are better equipped.

The believers are unaffected by this, because they are aware of the real cause and effect functioning of the world. And this reality tells them that victory has nothing to do with superiority in numbers or strength, but with the command and will of Allah. Indeed, true religion has to its credit many victories of faith: "How often, by Allah's will, has a small force vanquished a big one? Allah is with those who steadfastly persevere." *(Surat al-Baqara, 2:249)* It is pure faith that leads to victory. This mysterious truth, which cannot be understood by unbelievers, is explained in the verse below:

"O you who believe! When you meet a force, be firm, and call Allah in remembrance much (and often), that you may prosper."(Surat al-Anfal,8:45)

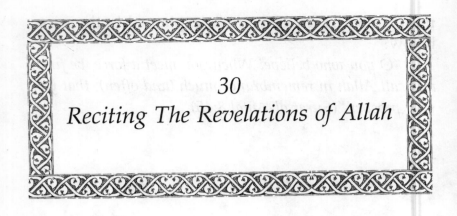

30
Reciting The Revelations of Allah

As expressed in the 7th verse of the 73rd Surah (*al-Muzzammil*), there are prolonged occupations in the day time for the believers. Surely, these occupations are for the benefit of religion even if they may require the believers to function in irreligious environments, becoming involved in profane societies.

Even in the midst of these worldly affairs the believers keep their faith in Allah and never lose sight of the spiritual point of view.

"Men whom neither trade nor sale can divert from the remembrance of Allah, nor from regular prayer, nor from the practice of regular charity. Their (only) fear is for the Day when men's hearts and eyes will overturned (from horror)" (Surat an-Nur, 24:37)

An important aspect of this virtue is keeping the revelations of Allah in mind. In the Qur'an, this important practice is emphasised in the following verse: "And recite what is revealed to you in your homes, of the Signs of Allah and His Wisdom: for Allah understands the finest mysteries and is well-acquainted (with them)." (*Surat al-Ahzab*, 33:34). As long as believers keep the Qur'an's verses in mind, they will correctly construe their manifestations in daily life and, in consequence, will feel closer to Allah.

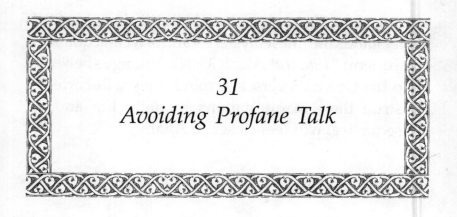

31
Avoiding Profane Talk

Believers are not interested in profane and useless talk and affairs. They find no satisfaction in such things and for them they are without value. They become involved in worldly affairs only if some benefit is to accrue to the cause of Allah. That is why believers are described in Qur'an as those "who avoid vain talk." (*Surat al-Mumenoon*, 23:3)

The above verse emphasizes that when a believer comes in contact with profane talk or events, he should turn his back and do something else useful for the divine Cause. This is the right behavior to please Allah. In order to do this, the believers should always be cautious, and know what they are doing. It would not be appropriate for a believer to argue with ignorant and shallow people except where some gain is to be achieved for the Cause. The Qur'an explains the ideal manner:

"When they hear vain talk, they turn away therefrom

and say: 'To us our deed and to you yours; peace be to you: we seek not the ignorant.'" (Surat al-Qasas, 28:55)

"They who do not bear witness to what is false, and when they pass by what is vain, they pass by nobly." (Surat al-Furqan, 25:72)

When a believer becomes free from his current work, he should continue with another useful task. As the verse explains: "Therefore, when you are free (from your immediate task), still labour hard, And to your Lord turn (all) your attention." *(Surat al-Inshirah, 94:7-8)*

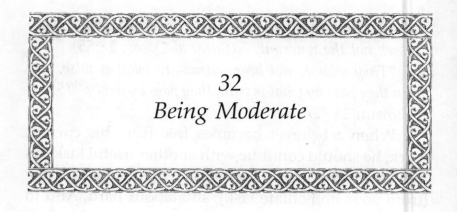

32
Being Moderate

To be moderate necessitates behaviour which remains within the boundaries of the Qur'an: that is, doing what is lawful and avoiding what is forbidden. This requires a well-balanced outlook. When believers become involved with profane societies, they should never act as their members do. Believers should always obey what has been decreed by the Qur'an, remaining consistently temperate in their approach.

However, this is definitely not something to be done just when the believers are in a society other than their own; they should also be of the same temper among the believers. There are also some situations when special attention should be paid to propriety:

"O you who believe! Do not raise your voices above the voice of the Prophet, nor speak aloud to him in talk as you may speak aloud to one another, lest your deeds become vain and you perceive not." (Surat al-Hujraat, 49:2)

Moreover, the risk of behaving immoderately

may even occur in doing something which is legitimate. This is because not every manner fits every situation. A way of speaking or behaving may sometimes be "unsuitable" or "improper" although it is not forbidden. That is why the believer should avoid being sharp-tongued or indulging in any other extremes of behaviour. He should try to develop his personality so as not to become nervous or very excited, and should never lose his temper or misbehave. The Qur'an expresses disapproval of conduct which is not consistently marked by moderation:

"No misfortune befalls on the earth or in yourselves but is inscribed in the Book of Decrees, before We bring it into existence. Verily, that is easy for Allah. In order that you may not despair over matters that pass you by, nor exult over favours bestowed upon you. For Allah does not love any vainglorious boaster." (Surat al-Hadid, 57:22-23)

33
The Angels Are Witness

People think that they are "all alone" if they are not seen by others. However, this is not really true. First of all, Allah is always with us, and sees and hears everything we do. Moreover, there are also invisible witnesses beside us who never leave us. These are the angels assigned to be our guardians, who record everything we do. The Qur'an informs us about this mystery:

"It was We Who created man, and We know what dark suggestions his soul makes to him: for We are nearer to him than (his) jugular vein. Behold, two (guardian angels) appointed to learn (his doings and note them), one sitting on the right and one on the left. Not a word does he utter but there is a sentinel by him, ready (to note it) (Surah Qaf, 50:16-18)

What is noted down by these angels shall be revealed on the Day of Judgment, when people will be interrogated about their deeds on earth. The Qur'an explains what will happen on that day:

"Then he who is given his book in his right hand, soon will his account be taken by an easy reckoning, and he will return to his people, rejoicing! But he who is given his book behind his back, soon will he cry for perdition and he will enter a blazing fire. Truly he lived among his people (in the world), rejoicing! Truly he thought that he would not have to return to Us! Nay, for his Lord was (ever) watchful of him!" (Surat al-Inshiqaq, 84:7-15)

34
Writing Down Transactions

People, by nature, are forgetful. That is why Allah commands the believers to write down transactions between them in the presence of witnesses:

"O you who believe! when you deal with each other in contracting a debt for a fixed time, then write it down; and let a scribe write it down between you with fairness; and the scribe should not refuse to write as Allah has taught him, so he should write; and let him who owes the debt dictate, and he should be careful of (his duty to) Allah, his Lord, and not diminish anything from it; but if he who owes the debt is unsound in understanding, or weak, or (if) he is not able to dictate himself, let his guardian dictate with fairness; and call in to witness from among your men two witnesses; but if there are not two men, then one man and two women from among those whom you choose to be witnesses, so that if one of the two errs, the second of the two may remind the other; and the witnesses should not refuse when they are summoned; and be not averse to writing it (whether it is) small or large,

with the time of its falling due; this is more equitable in the sight of Allah and assures greater accuracy in testimony, and the nearest (way) that you may not entertain doubts (afterwards), except when it is ready merchandise which you give and take among yourselves from hand to hand, then there is no blame on you in not writing it down; and have witnesses when you barter with one another, and let no harm be done to the scribe or to the witness; and if you do (it) then surely it will be a transgression in you, and be careful of (your duty) to Allah, Allah teaches you, and Allah knows all things." (Surat al-Baqara, 2:282)

In another verse, it is stated that it would be better to remit debts:

"If the debtor is in difficulty, grant him time till it is easy for him to repay. But if you remit it by way of charity, that is best for you if you only knew." (Surat al-Baqara, 2:280)

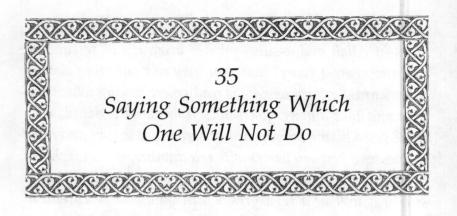

35
Saying Something Which One Will Not Do

Believers are obligated to keep their promises, just as decreed in the Qur'an: "Fulfill (every) engagement, for (every) engagement will be enquired into (on the Day of Reckoning)." (*Surat al-Isra*, 17:34)

Being trustworthy is one of the foremost characteristics of the believers. All the messengers have proved their righteousness to their people and been know as trustworthy and decent people. Fulfilling every engagement is a significant part of this trustworthiness.

Believers should keep their promises, and never commit themselves to anything which they think they will not be able to fulfill. It is said in the Qur'an as follows:

"O you who believe, why do you say that which you do not do? Greviously odious is it in the sight of Allah that you say that you do not do." (Surat as-Saff, 61:2-3)

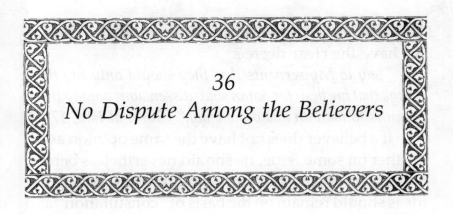

36
No Dispute Among the Believers

One of the secrets of the believers' success is the warm brotherhood and solidarity among them. The Qur'an emphasizes the importance of unity: "Truly, Allah loves those who fight in His Cause in battle array as if they were a solid cemented structure." (*Surat as-Saff*, 61:4)

Any statement or behaviour that may damage this close brotherhood would be an adversary act against religion itself. Allah warns the believers against this threat in the Qur'an:

"Obey Allah and His Messenger; and fall into no disputes, lest you lose heart and your power depart; and be patient and persevering: for Allah is with those who patiently persevere." (Surat al-Anfal, 8:46)

Hence, the sincere believer must be extremely cautious of entering into such disputes, avoiding words or manners that may hurt his brothers. Moreover, he should behave in such as way as to increase affection and confidence among them. In the Qur'an, we have the clear decree:

"Say to My servants that they should only say those things that are best: for Satan sows dissensions among them: Satan is to man an avowed enemy." (Surat al-Isra, 17:53)

If a believer does not have the same opinion as his brother on some issue, he should nevertheless behave and talk in the most modest and humble way. Sharing ideas should remain on the basis of "consultation" and not "debate". If a contention is observed among two other believers, then what one should do is indicated in the verse below:

"The believers are but a single Brotherhood. So make peace and reconciliation between your two (contending) brothers; and fear Allah, so that you may receive His Mercy." (Surat al-Hujraat, 49:10)

It should be noted that even a minor argument of any kind may have very negative effects on the Cause.

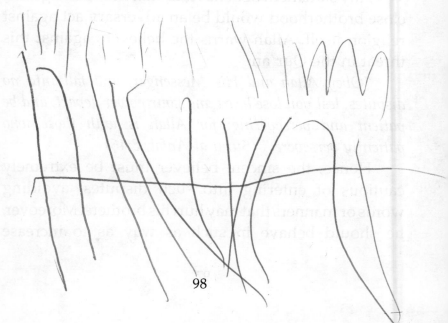

37
Seeking Allah's Protection from Satan While Reading the Qur'an

The Qur'an is the divine book revealed by Allah to guide mankind. While it helps increase the faith of the believers, it exposes the denial of the unbelievers.

"He it is Who has sent down to thee the Book: In it are verses basic or fundamental (of established meaning); they are the foundation of the Book: others are allegorical. But those in whose hearts is perversity follow the part thereof that is allegorical, seeking discord, and searching for its hidden meanings, but no one knows its hidden meanings except Allah. And those who are firmly grounded in knowledge say: 'We believe in the Book; the whole of it is from our Lord:' and none will grasp the Message except men of understanding." (Surat Aal-e-Imran, 3:7)

That means that some verses of the Qur'an have the capacity both to reveal the transgressions of "those whose hearts are flawed by perversity" and to increase the faith and submission of the believers.

99

It should be noted, however, that no one can guarantee that he will continue to preserve his faith. Believers may also lose the Qur'anic point of view with the effect of Satan's temptations. Naturally they would not perceive the wisdom in the Qur'an if they read it while under the sway of Satan. That is why Allah commands believers to seek refuge in Him from the evil influence of Satan before reading the Qur'an: "When you read the Qur'an, seek Allah's protection from Satan, the rejected one." (*Surat an-Nahl*, 16:98)

This command of Allah is important for it reminds believers of Satan's constant presence and unceasing activities. Indeed, Satan is ever at work, lying in wait for people on Allah's straight path, and trying to assault them "from before and behind, from their right and from their left." The strategies of Satan have been explained in many verses of the Qur'an. Thus salvation from the deceits of Satan can be achieved only through the Qur'an, which warns us against Satan's tricks and tells us to avoid them. As expressed in the 42nd verse of *Surat al-Hijr*, "Satan has no authority over Allah's servants." The solution is to accept the Qur'an as the only guide and to read it after seeking refuge in Allah from the rejected Satan.

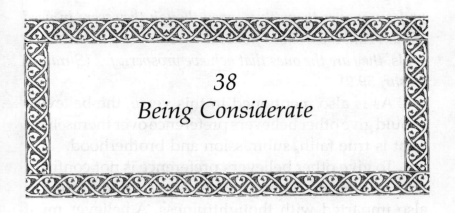

38
Being Considerate

The members of a profane society are, in the main, rude, uncaring and inconsiderate. The reason for this is the egoism of the unbelievers. They all think of their own benefit. Others have no importance for them.

However, a real group of believers are completely different from such people, because one of the significant characteristics of the believers is their refusal to fall a prey to their own greed. Believers who overcome their vain desires, will naturally be caring and considerate towards other believers. The Qur'an tells of that kind of self-sacrificing relationship between the refugees who fled with Mohammed to Medina and the faithful people of Medina who helped them:

"And those who, before them, had homes (in Al-Madinah) and had adopted the Faith, love those who emigrate to them, and entertain no desire in their hearts for things given to the (latter), and give them (emigrants)

preference over themselves, even though they were in need of that. And those saved from the covetousness in their own souls, they are the ones that achieve prosperity. " (Surat al-Hashr, 59:9)

As is also mentioned in this verse, the believers should give other believers preference over themselves. That is true faith, submission and brotherhood.

To give other believers preference is not confined only to offering them physical terms. Brotherhood is also imparted with thoughtfulness. A believer must consider the needs and problems of his brother more than those of himself.

Rude and inconsiderate manners show the insufficiency of a person's faith. A person who is not able to consider how his acts will affect the other believers, and who acts only according to his own "wishes" and "as he likes", is far removed from the example of the believer depicted by Allah. The Qur'an emphasizes this subject with many examples of both considerate and inconsiderate actions. And the most important is surely to be gracious and respectful to Allah's Messenger:

"O you who believe, do not put yourselves forward before Allah and His Messenger; but fear Allah: for Allah is He Who hears and knows all things." (Surat al-Hujraat, 49: 1)

"O you who believe, do not enter the Prophet's houses-until leave is given you- for a meal (and then) not (so early as) to wait for its preparation: But when you are invited, enter; and when you have taken your meal, disperse, without

102

seeking familiar talk. Such (behaviour) annoys the Prophet: he is ashamed to dismiss you, but Allah is not ashamed (to tell you) the truth. When you ask (his wives) for anything you want, ask them from behind a curtain: that is purer for your hearts and for their hearts. Nor is it right for you that you to cause annoyance to the messenger of Allah, nor that you should ever marry his wives after him. Truly, such a thing is in Allah's sight an enormity." (Surat al-Ahzab, 33:53)

People who are reared on the teachings of the Qur'an are noble, polite, upright and considerate. This is the natural attitude of the believer who gives preference to his brothers over himself and who feed for the love of Allah, the indigent, the orphan and the captive. Being considerate is a characteristic of the companions of Paradise. For instance; not disturbing a brother while he is on an important task, keeping silent when believers pray, making the believers as comfortable as possible, asking if they need something and serving them without being asked may be given as examples to kind behaviour. However, these are only a few examples, and these considerate manners may amount to hundreds and thousands according to changing conditions.

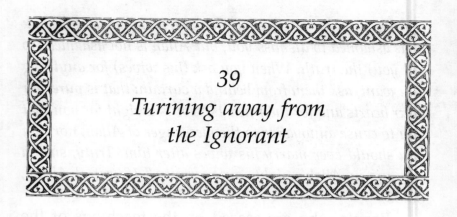

39
Turining away from the Ignorant

In the Qur'an, the believers are described as in the verses below:

"The servants of Allah (Most Gracious) are those who walk on the earth in humility, and when the ignorant address them, they say, Peace!'" (Surat al-Furqan, 25:63)

"And when they hear vain talk, they turn away therefrom and say: 'To us our deed and to you yours; peace be to you: we seek not the ignorant.'" (Surat al-Qasas, 28:55)

Believers are innately peaceful, whereas those who disbelieve are extremely uneasy, restless and aggressive. It is as if their torment of hell had already started on earth. That is why they cause trouble and are also constantly faced with difficulties. However, believers do not even communicate with those people unless they attempt to give harm to the believers and Islam. They behave honorably, as the above verses describe. When intervention is necessary, they do not behave rudely, but in the most civilized and law-abiding way.

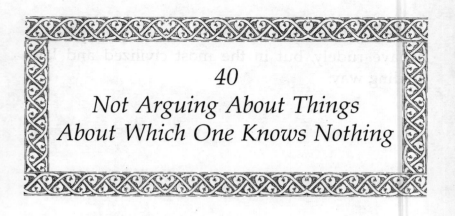

40
Not Arguing About Things
About Which One Knows Nothing

In the Qur'an, man is typified as being "contentious in most things." *(Surat al-Kahf,* 18:54) In other verses, this criticism is levelled particularly at the unbelievers:

"When (Jesus) the son of Mary is held up as an example, behold, your people raise a clamour thereat (in ridicule)! And they say: 'Are our gods best or he?' This they set forth to you, only by way of disputation. Nay! they are a contentious people." (Surat az-Zukhruf, 43:57-58)

The reason for this tendency to argue about everything is not to reveal and evaluate different opinions, but to satisfy the urge to quarrel. In the arguments of the ignorant, neither side tries to evaluate the others' ideas or find a correct solution. Beating the other is the one and only aim. This explains the loud voices and the tense attitude during such arguments, and the turning of what should merely be a discussion into a quarrel.

It is most abnormal surely, to argue over things about which neither disputant has any certain knowledge. The most obvious example of this is to be seen in discussions of religion, about which the arguers are generally exceedingly ignorant. The error of such conduct is pointed out in the verse below:

"Verily, you are those who have disputed about that of which you have knowledge. Why do you then dispute concerning that which you have no knowledge? It is Allah Who knows, and you know not." (Surat Aal-e-Imran, 3:66)

41
No Mocking

The following verse clearly tells us that there should be no mockery among the believers:

"O you who believe! Let not some men among you laugh at others: It may be that the (latter) are better than the (former): Nor let some women laugh at others: It may be that the (latter) are better than the (former): Nor defame nor be sarcastic to each other, nor call each other by (offensive) nicknames: Ill-seeming is a name connoting wickedness, (to be used of one) after he has believed: And those who do not repent are (indeed) doing wrong." (Surat al-Hujraat, 49:11)

Allah tells people to refrain from mocking. Mockery can take many forms: open laughter at personal misadventures, sly grins, verbal teasing under the pretence of joking, or sidelong glances to convey something which cannot be openly discussed. Such behaviour belongs to the culture of the ignorant and does not befit true believers. The Qur'an tells us that people who indulge in such behaviour will have to suffer the Fire of Allah mounting on to their hearts.

"Woe to every (kind of) scandal-monger and backbiter, who piles up wealth and keeps on counting it, thinking that his wealth would make him last for ever. By no means! He will be sure to be thrown into the crushing Fire. And what will make you know what the crushing Fire is? It is the Fire of Allah kindled (to a blaze), which mounts to the hearts of men: Surely it shall be closed over upon them, (they will be punished) in columns outstretched." (Surat al-Humaza, 104:1-9)

It is not possible for a believer to behave in any cynical manner after he knows this clear decree of Allah. Indeed, no believer behaves in that way deliberately. However, if ever a believer slips into that manner, he may be unaware of his wrong conduct and taking it as fun. But whenever he realizes that what he is doing is wrong, he should immediately stop and repent.

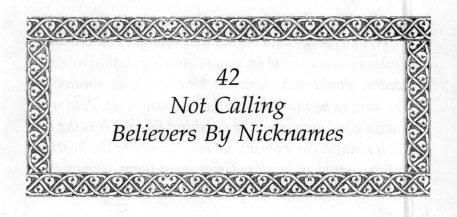

42
Not Calling
Believers By Nicknames

It is the habit of unbelievers to call each other by offensive nicknames. The idea behind it is again to humiliate others and to "prove" one's own superiority. The nickname may call attention to a physical defect or to past errors. The unbelievers do not forget wrongdoing and always remind the person of his mistakes, although he may not ever have repeated them.

However, believers are different from them. They are forgiving, and there is a close brotherhood among them; they do not stoop to behave in this way. Moreover, Allah has ordered the believer neither to "defame nor be sarcastic to one another, nor call each other by (offensive) nicknames." (*Surat al-Hujraat,* 49:11)

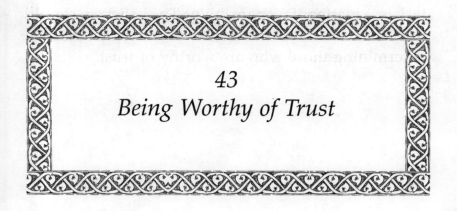

43
Being Worthy of Trust

The Qur'an describes the rendering back one's trusts to those to whom they are due as a moral principle and a way to success. Believers should always respect the trust reposed in them and thus win others' confidence in return. Besides, believers should also determine to whom to hand the trusts, that is, to whom they are due. On this, the Qur'an delivers the following injunction:

"Allah commands you to render back your trusts to those to whom they are due; and when you judge between man and man, that you judge with justice: Verily how excellent is the teaching which He gives you! For Allah is He Who hears and sees all things." (Surat An-Nisa, 4:58)

Another verse states.

"Whoever fulfills his promise and guards (against evil) - then surely Allah loves those who guard (against evil)." (Surat Aal-e-Imran, 3:76)

A trust may be something of financial value, or a

task or a matter of responsibility. The believers should use their wisdom and sense of discrimination in determining those who are worthy of trust.

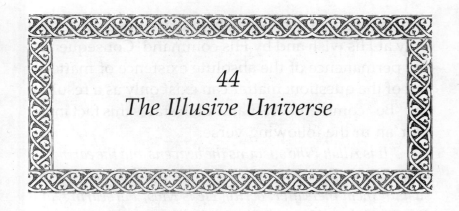

44
The Illusive Universe

A major flaw in any society which is ignorant of the precepts of Islam is its members' view that the material world they touch and see is the greatest and most absolute actuality of our earthly existence. In fact, they reckon that matter has an "eternal and never-ending" existence. Eventually, they start to deify matter, and seek help only from it. Consequently, they start to think of Allah less and less and even deny His existence. Their perception of Allah is of a "less realistic and more imaginary" being when compared to matter. However, this is a great misconception on the part of the unbelievers. The absolute being is not matter, but Allah. The Qur'an is quite specific on this point:

"That is because Allah is the Reality; and those besides Him whom they invoke are but vain Falsehood: verily Allah is He, Most High, Most Great." (Surat al-Hajj, 22:62).

In truth, matter has the ability to exist only so long

as it has been created by Allah. Its existence is preserved only at His wish and by His command. Consequently, the permanence of the absolute existence of matter is out of the question: matter can exist only as a result of the "Be" command of Allah. Allah states this fact in the Qur'an in the following verse:

"It is Allah Who sustains the heavens and the earth, lest they cease to function: and if they should fail, not one can sustain them thereafter: verily, He is Most Forbearing, and Oft-Forgiving. (Surat Fat'r, 35:41)

This means the complete world exists only with the sustanence of Allah and when He so orders, it shall cease to exist. In fact, this means that the entire universe is made of illusive matter, which will end when commanded. This boundless will of Allah is beyond comprehension, but dreams may be a way of understanding this creation to a certain extent. For instance, when someone wakes up from a dream, the universe which existed with all its details in the dream will fade from existence and disappear since the reason for that universe's existence is only one's own mind during sleep. When the mind stops "forming" such a universe, it suddenly "disappears," and does not exist anymore. Surely it had no material or independent being at all.

The prominent Islamic scholar, Imam Rabbani, narrates this absolute truth (the narration has been simplified and re-worded in translation):

"Allah has determined the reflection of each one of His names (the Just, the often returning, the Compassionate,

etc.) and has given His attributes to the created ones. And the beings for this reflection were created out of sheer nothingness. The One and Only Allah with His Power decreed a place of realization for His names and created them in the illusive (imaginary, supposed) universe. Moreover, He did this in the time and shape He wanted.

The existence of the universe is only in the illusive and sensational state and not in externality. In this case this is a permanence in nothingness and the illusive gains strength and soundness with the creation of Allah. So, the created becomes alive, knowing, doing, asking, seeing, hearing and speaking to the extent of His will. However, because of its being a reflection and having only a shadow existence, there is no trace of it externally. In the outside world, there is nothing other than Allah's Being and His names.

Everything has appeared on the mirror of the Superior Being and in this way, they have acquired an external appearance: they have looked as if existent in the outside world. But there is nothing other than this on the outside. There is no one and nothing but Allah." (Mektubati Rabbani, Imam Rabbani, p.517-519)

Since there is no being other than Allah and everything in the universe is a manifestation of His Being, then the author of all deeds is again the Almighty. In the Qur'an this secret is revealed in a number of verses:

"It was not you who slew them; it was Allah: when you threw a handful of dust, it was not your act, but Allah's: in order that He might test the Believers by a gracious trial from Himself: for Allah is He Who hears and knows all

things." (Surat al-Anfal, 8:17)

"But you will not, except as Allah wills; for Allah is full of Knowledge and Wisdom." (Surat al-Insan, 76:30)

"Remember when you met, He showed them to you as few in your eyes, and He made you appear contemptible in their eyes so that Allah might accomplish a matter already enacted. For to Allah do all questions go back for decision." (Surat al-Anfal, 8:44)

The world has an immanent face as well as an evident one. In the evident, everything looks to be independent and uncontrolled. However, in the immanent, in accordance with their illusory creation, everything has bowed to Allah's will. With the words of the Qur'an;

"I put my trust in Allah, my Lord and your Lord! There is not a moving creature, but He has grasp of its fore-lock. Verily, it is my Lord Who is on a straight path" (Surah Hud, 11:56)

Knowing that there is nothing other than Allah, unveils the secret reality that no one can do anything by himself. This secret should always be in the minds of the believers. Accordingly, the believers know that all perversions and misdeeds of the unbelievers are again decreed by Allah. Believers, therefore, interpret and evaluate all happenings according to their immanent implication. This helps them to do right, and to behave in a way which is most sincere, heedful, and wise.

They said: "Glory to You, of knowledge
We have none, save what
You have taught us: In truth it is
You Who are perfect in knowledge and
wisdom."
(Surat al-Baqara, 2:32)

Tabligh Movement

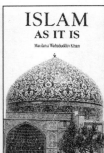

ISLAM
AS IT IS
Maulana Wahiduddin Khan

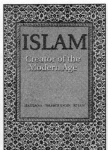

ISLAM
Creator of the Modern Age

MAULANA WAHIDUDDIN KHAN

Living Islam
TREADING THE PATH OF THE IDEAL

RUQAIYYAH WARIS MAQSOOD

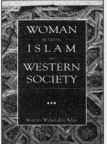

WOMAN
BETWEEN
ISLAM
AND
WESTERN
SOCIETY
...
Maulana Wahiduddin Khan

WOMAN
IN ISLAMIC SHARI'AH
Maulana Wahiduddin Khan

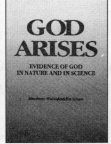

GOD
ARISES
EVIDENCE OF GOD
IN NATURE AND IN SCIENCE

Maulana Wahiduddin Khan

Introducing
Islam
A Simple Introduction to Islam

Maulana Wahiduddin Khan

THE INTRODUCTION TO ISLAM SERIES 1
THE
WAY TO
FIND GOD
Maulana Wahiduddin Khan

THE INTRODUCTION TO ISLAM SERIES 2
THE
TEACHINGS
OF ISLAM
Maulana Wahiduddin Khan

THE INTRODUCTION TO ISLAM SERIES 3
THE
GOOD LIFE
Maulana Wahiduddin Khan

THE INTRODUCTION TO ISLAM SERIES 4
THE
GARDEN OF
PARADISE
Maulana Wahiduddin Khan

THE LIFE OF THE PROPHET
MUHAMMAD
MUHAMMAD MARMADUKE PICKTHALL

The
Beautiful
Promises of
Allah
RUQAIYYAH WARIS MAQSOOD

The
Soul
of the
Qur'an
INSPIRING PRAYERS TO KINDLE
HEART AND MIND

SANIYASNAIN KHAN

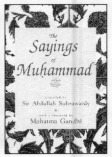

The
Sayings
of
Muhammad

Sir Abdullah Suhrawardy

with a foreword by
Mahatma Gandhi

ISLAM AND THE DIVINE COMEDY

MIGUEL ASIN

HARUN YAHYA

EVER THOUGHT ABOUT THE TRUTH?

THE MORAL VALUES OF THE QURAN

HARUN YAHYA

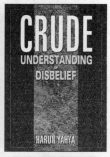

CRUDE UNDERSTANDING OF DISBELIEF

HARUN YAHYA

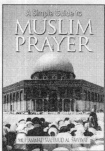

A Simple Guide to MUSLIM PRAYER

MUHAMMAD MAHMUD AL-SAWWAF

A Simple Guide to ISLAM

FARIDA KHANAM

A Simple Guide to ISLAM'S CONTRIBUTION TO SCIENCE AND CIVILISATION

MAULVI ABDUL KARIM

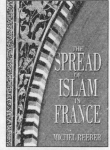

THE SPREAD OF ISLAM IN FRANCE

MICHEL REEBER

The Essential Arabic

A Learner's Practical Guide

Rafi'el-Imad Faynan

A HISTORY OF ARABIC LITERATURE

CLEMENT HUART

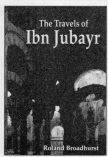

The Travels of Ibn Jubayr

Roland Broadhurst

THE STORY OF ISLAMIC SPAIN

SYED AZIZUR RAHMAN

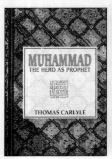

MUHAMMAD THE HERO AS PROPHET

THOMAS CARLYLE

THE ISLAMIC ART OF PERSIA

A.J. ARBERRY

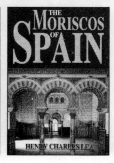

THE MORISCOS OF A SPAIN

HENRY CHARLES LEA

MUHAMMAD A PROPHET FOR ALL HUMANITY

MAULANA WAHIDUDDIN KHAN

The Qur'an
An Abiding Wonder
MAULANA WAHIDUDDIN KHAN

The Qur'an
T.B. IRVING

THE
KORAN

THE
QUR'AN
FOR
ALL HUMANITY
Maulana Wahiduddin Khan

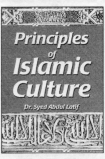

Principles
of
Islamic
Culture
Dr. Syed Abdul Latif

Selections
from the
Noble Reading
An Anthology of Passages from the Quran
T.B. IRVING

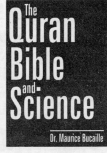

The
Quran
Bible
and
Science
Dr. Maurice Bucaille

A HISTORY OF
ARABIAN MUSIC
HENRY GEORGE FARMER

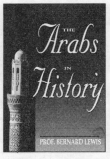

THE
Arabs
IN
History
PROF. BERNARD LEWIS

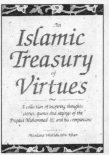

An
Islamic
Treasury
of
Virtues
A collection of inspiring thoughts,
stories, quotes and sayings of the
Prophet Muhammad ﷺ and his companions
Maulana Wahiduddin Khan

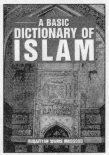

A BASIC
DICTIONARY OF
ISLAM
RUQAIYYAH WARIS MAQSOOD

THE MORAL
VISION
Islamic Ethics for Success in Life
Maulana Wahiduddin Khan

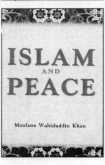

ISLAM
AND
PEACE
Maulana Wahiduddin Khan

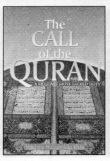

The
CALL
of the
QURAN
A MUSLIM'S MOST SACRED DUTY

The
Muslim
Marriage
Guide
Ruqaiyyah Waris Maqsood

Uniform Civil Code
A Critical Study
Maulana Wahiduddin Khan